Train
River
Poetry

anthology

www.trainriver.org

Follow us on Instagram @train_river_publishing

Dedication

This book is dedicated
to those who encourage us
and pick us up when
we fall.

Foreword

Welcome to our Summer 2021 Poetry Anthology. We are overjoyed to present this long awaited edition.

Many events have passed since these poems were first brought to life by their poets. We have collectively experienced changes from AI, Roe v. Wade, and Twitter, to Queen Elizabeth II, Wordle, and the Choco Taco. New wars started, and old wars continued.

We invite you back in time with us to the Summer of 2021. NFTs and Covid-19 are going strong. The postponed 2020 Summer Olympics and Paralympics are hosted in Tokyo. Derek Chauvin is convicted. Canadian wildfires blaze, and Europe floods. Sea Shanties trended on TikTok.

In a way, this edition has already withstood the test of time, certainly much better than the headlines and trends. The beauty, love, joy, loneliness, comfort, ennui, and wit of these poems are as vivid today as ever. We hope you enjoy.

Love always,

Train River Publishing

Thank You

We would like to extend a special thank you to our incredible Supporting Members who make our publications here at Train River Publishing possible. With their support we have been able to provide low barrier to entry opportunities for poets and writers from around the world.

Thanks to our Supporting Members, and readers like you, we are able to offer all of our programs for free. Our books are available to borrow from libraries around the world so everyone can enjoy our publications.

We have also been able to launch a free Chapbook Workshop at trainriver.org to teach writers and poets how to create, design, publish, and market chapbooks. This program is designed with all audiences in mind and is geared to give a writer all the tools and insight they need to bring their vision to life.

We are grateful for the support of our community and are looking forward to continuing to create more opportunities for years to come.

Supporting Members

Timothy Haywood

Rosmarie Schaut

Jacqueline Collins

Elizabeth Hefner

Les Brown

Jim Chisholm

Ashok Karnak, MD

Alinda Wasner

Catherine Hamilton

Rosalyn Goodridge

Judith A Vaughn

Steven Piekutoski

Darlene Ealy

Karen Haefelein

David Parker

Alan Abrams

Daniel Doeden

Joan Gerstein

CEC Haydon

Leon Gregori

Marie Claire

Katherine Palmer

Marcella Cavallo

Michael R Mac Donald

Ellen Rogers

Marianne Gambaro

Edison Jennings

Libby Chandler

Leon Dunne

Michael Ware

David Stant

Sandra Noel

Patrick Connors

Andy Baldwin

David Ament

Don Thompson

David Avila

Mark Stein

thewhite.m05

Sam Piscitelli

Dakota Avellino

TazThePoet

Supporting Members

Barbara Soehner

Alex Henderson

Nancy Next

R.H. Alexander

Jacqueline Olivia

Christopher Woods

Ashok Karnik, MD

David Coy

Jim

Michael MacDonald

Kirsten Morgan

Mallory Abreu

Annie Percik

Lana Hechtman Ayers

Stephanie Robertson

William Falo

Karl Kadie

KC

Tanja Krstulovic

Amelia Robyn

Jarrius Smith

David Lott

Anonymous

Rosemarie Schaut

Liz Mercedes

Dr. Joyce C. Brown

Katherine Palmer

Doris Ferleger

John Mueter

MCPoesia

Ana Dee

Eileen Wiscombe

Jenni Jolly

Lauren Michelle

Sian Maciejowski

Marcia Knight-Latter

Elizabeth

Jessica

Jessica Bullard

James Goggin

and the
Filipino Artists Association of Sweden

Summer 2021

cities, skyscrapers, streets and daisies

Rocío Romero García

i saw a daisy in the middle of the road
surrounded by weeds and ants
and i was fascinated about how much life
the sidewalk had,
but a car parked during a summer evening
under the only shadow of the town
and squashed the flower and scared the ants
and suddenly the green was black,
i cried clouds
but the sun came up again
and the daisy revived more yellow that before
and i understood that it doesn't matter
how hard the concrete is
if you're stronger
than the gravel at your feet;
we are the flowers of every street
that weren't meant to be there.

@losmundosdero

Publication

James McNinch

As I sit by my window,
I recall the words I wrote as a child:

"Summery scenes in the summer sun.
Any watery days? None, none, none!"

Those words were true; I was
Carefree.
What changed?

I grew, yes,
Taller,
But more ambitious,
Daring,
Stronger.

Yet, also weaker. My ambition
Silenced by chloroform;
My daring
Haunted by home truths.

Those words were used in my first ever
Publication;
A noun, literally meaning
'To be published, or made public'.

Why those words?
Such sentiment is replaced nowadays by

"I cannot but drown
In rivers of sorrow
Flowing from my eyes."

As I sit by my window,
I recall the words I wrote as a child.

How I long to be ten years old again.

@james_mcninch

to play god...
John Stojevich

the earth
does not discriminate
against who can eat its food...

no, humans do that.

@johnstojevich

Hero of Color

Brendan De Lucia | Word.Bender

My olive skin provides me
with ample opportunities
to exploit my white privilege.
Depending on the hue of the
situation, I can portray any socially
accepted image. As a kid, I would
summon somber rain clouds in
ignorant attempts to wash away
my pigmentation. My uniqueness was
being falsely labeled as a natural violation.
As an adolescent, society introduced me
to pleasant antidepressants. Teaching me
lessons on how to suppress my intuitive
questions. As an adult, I have accepted
the opal dimensions of my multi-colored
reflection. I am a proud person of color
and I refuse to be lessened.

@Word.Bender

cinctura lilium

Caitlan Docherty

womb of mid-afternoon heat, pulse of strangers
thrumming, amorphous shapes in the sand.
unknowing becomes you, banded tulip;
i'll curl my ear in your forever
exhale if you'll promise
to shore my steely wanting, give it beach
glass glint; bright aqua, honey-amber,
citron, cornflower blue. the predetermined dusk
drags its purple tongue across dimming
sky, a residual kindness that lasts until sundown.

@cmnpoetry

Bathing In Plants

Howard Young

We sat in the garden cafe
Bathing in plants,
Hanging baskets like Babylon
Roof strung,
Hungry pigeons stare through glass
Cobbled brick pots dripping water
Licked up by the shadows
Drifting through.

The whole deal
Overpriced, and somehow sexy
Like Paris
Like the wine and the food
We are
Caught in the afternoon
(Like wild birds in haystack nets
My itinerant great great
Used to eat
As he wandered the country in eighteen something
Hanging from rope beds)
We cannot leave.

Renters looking for home cheer
Enter the stage,
Entertaining chats about
Bagging a dangling fuchsia
Iced buds and long leaves,
Trailing, the

Tall man sweeps it through the air
Takes him home
Like a magic broom.

Yet my wine still dries up,
Less than a sip left
Like a dead sea puddle in a dry spring
And something like wind
Pulls at my ankles,
I have grown this afternoon
On the inside
Or maybe just aged.

Now
Ready for the hill home,
And playing records
With Patti Smith
To shake out the ghosts
And the gathering dust of Cafe afternoons.

@brighton_typewriter_poet

Poem

Tom Beck

after W. H. Auden

He read with eyes of curiosity
How beetles fly, what ants and earwigs eat;
Overturned the rocks in his brain to see
What cracks lay hidden in the world's concrete;

And thinking, emerged from his confusion:
"All the cheerful naturalists have it wrong,
The dead, too, must add to this profusion,
And evolution is a mournful song."

At last, he saw things as they were, and stirred,
Went to the altar of the oaks to pray:
But, in the whisper of the leaves, he heard

A sound that sharpened in his nerves – a sword,
A disembodied voice in the dark midday
That cried and grew louder, yet said no word.

@tombeckwrites

Together, old we'll grow.

Simon E. Northcott

Somehow
I know
for sure,
we'll grow
old together:
all wrinkled
like those potatoes
we forgot to have,
bones as dry as
the Atacama desert,
and yet still beautiful
like when its dunes are
covered in pink flowers.

@simone.northcott

Sacred Moments

Judith Vaughn

Sacred Moments

show up, no announcement, no fanfare, no music.
One day I walk out the gate with my dog.
I look up the street, see the raccoon
lying in a puddle next to the road.

Dog barks, behind the gate now. My steps
hesitant toward the injured, maybe dead, animal.
She rests on her outstretched paws. Her
small tongue laps from the dirty pool that
holds yesterday's rain, and now her blood.

Stretching up on her front legs, she briefly
holds her masked pointed face to the sun.
The murky pool pulls her back to the depths.
Snout down in the muck, she lifts her head
again, snorts the water out her nose,
rests on her paws, looks at me.

My words of comfort are lost on her. She is dying.
Unexpectedly, she lifts her head for a last time,
looks up at me, then at the blue sky; stretches
her front legs. A deep sigh ripples down her lovely back.
Tears from her black eyes roll down her face.

This is the moment.
I am witness to her death. I honor her going.
Her silky fur shines in the mid-day sun
as the wind whispers through it. The caress
offers more comfort than my words,
something familiar, gentle.

I have witnessed other goings. My
heart swells; this is grace. Like birth,
both ordinary and profound.

@poemdawg

Astral Travel

Kelly Maida

Last night I traveled someplace else, while lying in bed.
Visions of an Oceanside house filled my head. Traveling by
the sea. My daughter and strange people were talking to
me! I heard the angel number 1065! Then a rabbit ran off,
not sure if he was dead or alive. But then I found the rabbit.
It was just fine. I gave it back to its owner, because it was
not mine. I think I traveled into the future and this was a
later date in time.

@kellymaida

Jessica Huddy

unattended in the kitchen you manage
over the dinner you cooked me

I am sinking ships
orbiting other planets
untenable in the truest sense

the moderate light
displays your mild manner
exposes my self-involvement

I think up ways to reimburse
your tolerance

but I don't have anything you're made of

@j.l.huddy

An era of love

Benerandakate

we took a polaroid of us, (that day!)
as keepsakes, on knowing that all of
the in betweens (between us)
cannot and (will not) last forever.

we were painters, who painted (that day!)
distinct hues of red and orange
and tainted shades of purple too
in the enchanting sky, up above.

through our dazed eyes and perplexed minds,
one can tell that back to back invisible love letters
have been written to one another, over many centuries ago
(just like the back of our hands) long before our own
journey
had even had the chance to begin.

t'is the story of how a boy met a girl, with eyes
as glistening as the sun, whose name as foretold,
was imprinted inside his heart forever, from the dawn of
time.
t'is the story of how a girl met a boy, with a
heart too pure for this datk world, who like a northern sky
could always find his way back to hers.
to only lead her back home safely time and time again
(somewhere in the distant sky,
echoed, a love story unlike any other.)

@benerandakate

A Self Portrait

Courtney Phillips

i am my own becoming and undoing. hazel eyes shine in the sunlight but they have not been bright in some time. liquid gold pours down my cheeks and leaves specks and freckles that have only grown tarnished. copper crumbs of dying constellations. my cheeks are full but i do not take the bites out of life that i wish to. they are empty other than my teeth, clenched shut and crooked at the front. i bite the hands that come too close, and kiss the hand that feeds me. i used to kiss hands that didn't, too. i learnt not to. there's only one cup and one spoon and one bowl that i like to use at home but i think we know by now that i have a picky appetite. my pockets on too-tight or too-baggy jeans are overflowing with dreams. my hands are ink and paint stained. my nails filled with dirt even when they are clean. i am a plant reaching from beneath the earth. reaching for sunlight and the release of rain. my ears are filled with distant birdsongs and sometimes they are overflowing too. i have trouble listening. eyes clouded over. the world moves faster than my hands can hold onto it. i drag memories with me, pulling them across the sky; cirrus clouds. i have trouble letting go. head in the clouds and feet six feet under. mind six feet under and filled with dark nights. press my pen to my pupil and find more ink to write. from my nose, more ink to write. i am terrified of dying. i am terrified of being forgotten. i have thrown myself into the arms of panic and only sometimes am i strong enough to step away. i am becoming- becoming- becoming- at the fastest pace i can carry. there is so much that i carry. i never thought that clouds would be this heavy. i am my own becoming and my own undoing.

@courtneyphillipsstorytelling

Pretend We Are Mountains

Devin McPherson

Let us pretend we are mountains,
Let us feel massive and timeless,
We have no memory of how we began,
And we have no concept of when we will end.

We are mountains that have streams,
Near our peaks we create rivers that flow powerfully and
uncontrolled in our youth.
Yes, even mountains were once young.

Such force makes our rivers change as time bends their flow
and creates lakes.
The water still flows but we hold a little back,
Still our river flows, it must never stop.

We are mountains filled with precious resources that can't be
replaced.
We trade them for things that will fade.
We will someday crumble from this forced exchange.

Forget those things, they were doomed to be taken from the
start.
All that matters is our rivers that we believe can give
continuously.

Let's pretend our rivers are love,
It pours from us without control and flows freely to those that
are near us.
We often forget as our river flows past our view it will
eventually reach everyone.

It will flow with other rivers to the ocean where it becomes
salty.
All love eventually ends in tears.

Think like a mountain.
Realize that the tears evaporate and nourish our peaks so that
our rivers can flow.

We are a world of mountains on a planet that is getting
warmer.
Mount Saint Helen reminds us that even mountains have a
temper.

Every day more mountains show their temper and warmth
becomes heat.
Heat fills our oceans, trapping the tears and our rivers become
weak.

Such heat could stop the flow till we are nothing but dry
rocks.
Waiting for the ocean to wear us down beneath waves of tears.

Let's pretend that we are always giving more than we receive.
Let's promise never to tell the other,
Because that's how love is supposed to work.

To Feast on Orange

Jenna Maria Todinovski

If I could visit a past life in this one dream
I'd remember the strawberry fields as the dessert that
came before the dinner. The Saturday drives down
unnamed dirt roads that brought us there. The simple
practice of our devotion steering us onward to greener
land, *or so we hoped*. It wasn't so tragic when the station
on the radio turned to static and then to silence. It was
the welcomed precipice of freedom. It was you and I as
naked as God intended.
It was the sun willfully melting. Blades of grass tenderly
bending. The heavenly clouds hanging low enough to
touch. It was extending beyond the fabric of land as much
as it was beyond the scale of ourselves. Summers and
sonnets of surrendering one vision for another. It was the
lifetimes you could live in one day; the choosing of a
moment and the moment it became a picnic. The blanket
our only sentiment of all that would unfold. Of the food
and laughter we'd share. The wine we'd pour and the
circling of time we'd eventually forget to count. The love
we'd make in the name of poetry.
Poetry, that's what we'd name the road in another life. And
the wildflowers in your hands were nothing like the
pretty lies that flowered after. *Lies needed more care.* So
we pursued devastation like a chance for parched mouths
to savour every last drop of wine. The soft peck of a
bruise- we drank to that. A piece of the earth wrecked

and worshipped- we drank to that. We drank to the pendulum of our bodies beating to a tireless drum.
We drank to the vision of us growing wilder and wilder. The echo of us growing louder and louder.
The fall from grace was dizzier than Van Gogh's swirling paint. Our shallow breaths filled with the regrettable taste of dinner fresh on our tongues. The violent nature in us debated slicing or tearing through bread with bare hands. We collected the tiny crumbs from our fight from before the drive down, until it was all we consumed. I could see those same hands banging on walls and their fists swelling, just as their hearts must have been. The pair that would bang every year *for one more year*. And the other pair that confused mercy for victory. I remembered wanting to paint over the pale orange you'd chosen for the dining room walls. *And what I'd give to feast my eyes on only orange. To peel its layers and pick its pieces and feel only you*. This is what war does, you'd tell me, as if following the script for every great war in history. You'd go on to tell me, as the paint slowly and painfully dried, we don't return to who we were before.
And if this revelation could shake every atom we are made of. If the Saturday we'd wake to wasn't the loose thread of our destiny. If loose threads didn't end picnics. If words had always been soft as petals you'd feel me nudge you awake to say-
my love, I'm on your side.

@withlove_maria.mena

Radical Acceptance

Serena Morrigan

I swore never to write again
Yet here I am, scribbling
Retelling the same old stories
This is what I do best
Because I cannot forget
Because I cannot let go
Accept life for what it is
Outrageous endeavour
I swore never to write again
Another broken promise

@serena.morrigan

a birthday blueprint

Caitlan Docherty

an omen backwards
   still good: funfetti cake and french

      rosé producing tangible proof with fire
         tearing across earth's surface

partitioning a singed sky—the reaper
   inhaling me at the horizon

      all my charred matter swept in luminous death
         breath to cull the imperfect self and awaken

spirit the anchoring root flowering topaz
   treetop high whole

      body glittering auspice grew
         wings to fly

@cmnpoetry

the kind of love that is beyond us

Yadawanka Pala

it rained for the first time today. i saw our shadows coming
back to life. how we used to stay up watching the same
movie over and over because you liked the way i laughed.
how the first picture we ever took was under the covers
because nobody was supposed to find out about us. i
remember exchanging notes at public places and walking
on different sides of the road. pretending we didn't plan to
enter the same shops on the way home. we were so caught
up in what we were able to give that we forgot we were
dealing with so much more. in time you became an
extension of me. i wouldn't have learned to take care of my
body if you have not taught me to love. i wouldn't have
been able to make it through the week if you didn't give me
reasons to stay. everything we've ever been through has
made a comeback. i now carry the weight of all five years
that you have been a part of. it's amazing how the both of
us, no matter how different are still able to be one. create
something bigger than the both of us. i look at you now and
see how much of myself you have become. you now make
playlists and order take out. things you would never have
agreed to. i now socialize and use words that are way out of
my comfort zone. learn to make you dinner while you bend
down to tie my shoes. buy you extra pillows because i've
never really needed one. get used to waking up every
morning and watch you snore. no more wishing the hours
could multiply while we facetime. no more hugs and kisses
through long emails we somehow never forget to send. now

my space has you in it and i've never been so happy to have someone be a part of me. of us.

@twit.terpatted

the evening of the incarcerated flowers.

Rocío Romero García

i went for a walk
after so long,
the sky said storm
but screamed it late enough
to let me see.
i saw flowers incarcerated
behind the bars of a private garden,
pigeons pecking a bottle of beer,
ripped posters out of fury and
contempt for the order,
terraces and glances
and couples with walking sticks
and no umbrellas,
dogs running after a ball
and a carousel spinning,
store windows and familiar smells
that made me turn and look
for a space that could give them a face,
streets with leaves and weeds
that made me think about
how it would be life in miniature;
everything would be more simple
if we reconsider the scale of our
problems.
i get into the library
and there was a suffocating atmosphere,
i've passed through the day with my heart
in quarantine and the whispers

and the heat made the books
try to eat me.
i got home and i lay in the bed
and i cried again,
i didn't know when it would stop,
maybe when the spring was over
and turned all the tears
in roses,
i don't know if it was of happiness
or distress,
of liberation or sadness
or comfort to know the ground didn't
open under my feet;
i've gone through the day with less noise,
but the noise still there.

@losmundosdero

Parsnips
L.G.Chandler

Roast potato crisp, enriched in oil
Cavities crunching into delicate insides
Complimented by slowly stewed, stripped
Carrots on the side,
Juicy beef submerged in smoothened gravy,
Not too thin, not too thick
A substantial grip,
Glances across the elongated, dining table
Both unsure of our place
Sharing shifty eye contact with each spoonful,
Then they would surface
The parsnips with their long noses,
Sweet but with an aftertaste of... Garden
Curtained with stiff, sewn edges
Rubbing against my tongue buds,
I hurried, breath held, swallowing each one
Because you'd worked all morning, head in the oven

It's not that I hate parsnips,
It's not that I hate you,
It's that I never really liked you,
Not in the slightest

@l.g.chandler

disbanding the boxed wine cult
Caitlan Docherty

October treetops glowing
>> orange in the too early AM. sleepless
>>> second day hangover after
more breakup sex glares.

>> my head, smacked
>>> w color bar test signals & basic
cable TV static,
>> fuzzes short term memory–
>>> mediocre post-love lovemaking

on acid. you, brushing your teeth
>> & pouring orange juice,
>>> you're the cheap earworm
i keep selling out for.

@cmnpoetry

This is a ghost story

Leonie Puschmann

I don't know how to say this
but I had a dream in which you died.
And ever since
I saw two versions of you, one hardly there and one alive.
I saw the world in a different light,
a vacant place, then blink, then see you standing there
right in front of me.
Cold shame.
I don't know how to phrase this
without sounding like a fraud.
I know that I'm a coward,
but I had a dream in which I had to me bold and strong and
fierce,
and all of the above
while also grieving.
Stripped.
Draped in a coat of black emotions.
And ever since I think, Am I not surrounded by ghosts?

While I came face to face with the remaining essence of
what you had been,
I saw myself, reflected in those hollow eyes,
and realized
that all my life I have always been a ghost.
Hardly there.
Sometimes so thin in spirit that I myself was not even aware
of my own presence.

So, I had a dream in which I died,
and only a ghost version remained,
haunting the earth and hunting the length of the world,
back and forth and back again
and when I fell back into the place that I had left
I saw
that everything was just the same.

@pretendingtoliveinanotherworld

WAITING

Barbara Soehner

Is there anything more uncomfortable than waiting
Waiting...such a helpless condition
We are all so trusting in this world
Really kind of helpless when it comes to our health
When someone else is in control

Surgeons are gifted and talented
They save lives
When it comes to removing rubbish from your body
Rubbish that suddenly appeared without warning

In my case it was scary to be cut open
                    Have things removed from my body, from
my soul
My uterus has been thrown away
There is an empty space inside me now

Empty inside
As a woman I want to know
What's going to happen next
Did the cancer disseminate
What stage is it in
There were two surgeons...one removed my lymph nodes
The other my Uterus
Apparently the lymph nodes hold the clues

There is no immediate answer
I've been told "you will have to wait till next week to see
the doctor"
Another seven days of not knowing where I am
Nothing I can do
Yeah...waiting really really hard
I'm not happy about it at all

Waiting has taken my hope
Made me scared...scared because
I don't know
What the answer will be

@barbara_soehner

Your Eyes

after Muskan Kashif, @m.k.poet

Skyler Saunders

you keep calling, and calling, but
the person you're trying to reach
hasn't existed for years. by now
you should be holding a funeral,
burying anything you ever hoped
for us, leaving whatever grave
you dig empty, empty, empty.
sometimes I am grateful that I
don't have your eyes; other times
the denial doesn't cut it and I'm
left bitter and seeing and stung.
other times I want to rip them
out, get colored contacts, fuck
the way you make me see myself.
I know good things can come
from bad. I know saying you're
the worst thing about me lets
me off too easy. I can be bad
on my own. I can still, even
without your eyes. even if we
looked like strangers.

@skyler.celeste.poetry

92129

Emily Sun Li

there's a scar on my heart
that traces the San Diego coastline
from the peach trees in your
best friend's backyard to the nude beach
in La Jolla we never explored

I can't tell if I'm still in love
with the pulse of your city or
if our blood just pumped faster
when we were teenagers fueled
by all-you-can-eat Korean barbeque,
weed we smoked on the playground
of your old elementary school, and
toxic romanticizations of codependency

either way, in another life I'll meet you
at our Mexican place--you grab the burritos,
I'll grab the limes and your left butt cheek
we'll head to the sea in your '99 Lexus
licking guac from each other's fingertips

sandy   naked   high
        on summer break
        and 18 forever

@poetry.by.e

6:30 pm on a summer night

Cyrus Ryan

I'm most comfortable in environments
Where the memories surround me
The people are gone
But the feelings aren't faded
Like a smiley face
Written on a mirror from the steam
Once the future becomes present
The past just feels like a dream

@csdevitt

Two in the Morning

C.c. McQ

You stumble home to me,
crawling into sheets we share,
smelling of sex and cigarettes.

"Where have you been?" I ask,
dodging whiskey-soaked
lips stained by another.

I watch the usual lies spew
from his overflowing cup.
"I had to work late," he slurs.

It's two in the morning,
and I say nothing at all.
It's two in the morning,

and there is nothing left to say.

@ccmcq_poetry

Vegetarian trip to the Carvery

Howard Young

At the pub carvery I make my way to the front of the queue and the chef, staring at my t shirt says to me "Vel-vet und-er-ground" who is that then?

What do you do? Try to explain the history of one of the worlds most influential collection of musical protagonists in some detail to a man who probably does not care, or give a brief ineffectual answer that sounds as if you do not even really know the answer to the question about your own t-shirt?

He has framed the question, he has control of the conversation. Whatever you say it will look ridiculous. To make matter worse you are a grown man and with your mum, and no-one here knows you are married with children, just some saddo who comes to lunch in a carvery with his mum, probably because he lives with her and has no friends, they unjustly suppose.

Either way he has drawn attention to you, the whole queue listens.

So you go for the brief answer "Some band from New York in the 1960's", you mumble as if admitting to some petty crime or other.

"Ohhhh" he says, his faint Brummie Birmingham sarcasm dripping like poisoned honey from his angled mouth.

Looking mockingly at the person behind you and raising one eyebrow he says "I see." He pauses for what seems like an hour, then "Which meat, turkey, pork or beef?" he drawls, exhaling with mock exasperation.

"Err... none please I am having the vegetarian carvery".

"Ohhh" he replies, and gives you a huge Yorkshire pudding as his idea of a consolation prize. He winks as he hands you your plate and your humiliation is complete. You bow your head as you gather vegetables and begin the walk of shame back to your table.

Meanwhile your mum looks down at the tiny pile of food she has gathered on her plate "I'll never eat all this," she says.

@brighton_typewriter_poet

Summer

Candela Rivero

It was summer
when you fell in love, it was summer
when the sun tickled our skin like butterfly kisses but
perhaps you confused the heat, the season
with love. It was summer
that held us together like melting
ice-cream hiding in the safety of your mouth,
but even summer comes to an end. When fall
arrived, our melted, merged lives drifted
away from each other.

@c.r.words

Cloud

Rosa G.

I am helplessly lost
in the grey clouds
finding my way through touch.
Fingers
stretched palm to palm,
the merest piece of sky held up
to my eyes
squeezed tight against the coming rain.
Aquarius rises and touches the sun
pulling me up to taste the air,
tumbling and moving in time
inside the fullness of leaden skies
which break and mumble,
the smallest shudder
until rain follows
drenching me and hollowing out my bones
that I might fly and land safely
back to earth,
where the clouds have names and
sky coloured eyes.

@rosa.g.words

THE DARK SIDE OF THE MOON KEEPS ME
PAINFULLY ALIVE

Seema Tabassum

rosewater resolutions were
too fragrant to stay unbroken,
raining red roses
didn't sustain the cause either,
the ceasing evening that is now February
was lost running for a cause
rendering me a lost cause,
a bored divergence
turned insignificant
turned towards you
towards death
I chose death
I chose death

the sun was such redundance
that I burned it up
and called it a night,
tribulation tripped on ink
and fell into a poem
I named the poem 'YOU,'
and got over it
(*or over you or did I?*),
now I'm waiting for March
to knock my nostrils and senses out
with the pollen it meticulously collects
from the fragrant flowers flooding the fields

I choose March
I choose March

the monumental regret
bestowed upon me for trying
to get over something
that keeps me alive,
grows hands
twists my arms
chokes me cordially;
I gamble
the dark side of the moon
a glinting delicacy
for momentary relief
I choose you
I choose you

I threw love out of the window,
and now I am crying about
living without hurt.
Is *dead* better than *excruciating*? ...

@seema_tabassum_poetry

Sonnet 28

Tom Beck

I want to cut you
free – fly north, my bird. I do not want
to see you every day. I do not want to summon

all these words. No wait –
it's better where you are, please stay.
I cannot see you
nor the winking stars
behind the clouded veil on which I write;
nor can the blazing insolence
of Mars contain
the blurry image I recite.
There is nothing

for me or you on earth.
Although you have no body,
cannot feel the breadth of centuries
before your birth, I have a voice
and I will let you steal

my life.
And though we cannot meet,
I'll wait,
and in my boredom, you
I will create.

@tombeckwrites

Morning coffee with a friend

Karina Kupp

Skipping breakfast at home. Feeling hungry, not exactly for food. The approaching change in the atmosphere. Anticipation. The air feels tastier. Not enough. Cappuccino and a pie. First sip. Stopping the time. Wherever I thought I needed to hurry up to be doesn't exist right now. Should it exist any time? Should I hurry at all? **Calmness.** Ideas. Life expectations. Exchange. Transformation. Not hope, but intention. Wordless. **Not saying much, more like having a series of life altering pauses. Change born in silences.** Simple words suddenly not sounding like a cliche, but having much more meaning. Hearing nothing but our own thoughts in a place that's not exactly that quiet. Weird. But **so clear**. Should I turn my life around completely when I walk out? At least to some extent. Excited to see how it turns out. Taking the longer route on the way home to make the mood stay longer. Using the energy before it's gone. Creating a real physical evidence of the morning.

The moment in time is art.

Art is the moment in time.

@mutedpoems

A table booked for two

Simon E. Northcott

Once I dined by myself
but I disguised my loneliness
behind a table booked for two:
on the back of the empty chair
in front of me, I gently put
a black tailleur I had bought
in a charity shop,

to the waiter who asked me
for the third time if everything
was ok and we were ready to order
I said that I had just been dumped,

he mumbled that he was sorry,
I shrugged my shoulders and nodded
thankful, in silence,

then I ordered a bottle of red wine
and I smiled daydreaming,
thinking about all the fights,
the memories, the life
we never had.

@simone.northcott

Resurrection

Elaine T. Stockdale

The winter sky could kill a man,
with just a single stare.
But the summer sun with its fierce kiss,
will bring him back to life.

@e.tstockdale_

OBNUBILATE

Michelle Nicole Gerrard

Violin strings.
The high pitched tone that sends shivers up and down the spine.
Each vibration mimicking the way your fingertips so gently grazed mine.
In a delicate dance of wanting and indifference.

As brief as Jasmine in the spring your arms wrapped around me.
Your scent lingering on the evening sky, a tapestry of cover that I could not for the life of me understand.
We were not the kind of love that was made of captivating shouts and song.
Rather a house of whispers and hushes.
Humble slivers of time where your hand would rest on the small of my back
Your eyes looking for mine even when I couldn't meet your gaze
Subtle nuances that lead to a collision of the high, bright, sweet melody of strings.
Sans souci.

Without worry.
In the scent of you, the presence of you.
The way even in the silence I could feel your heartbeat and it was steady as the flowing rivers.

I felt the clouds descend when you pulled away.

A constant cycle of leaning into the warmth and being burned by the frigid cold.
An illusion, to obnubilate my heart,
Somewhere between dreams of a blossoming love and a deafening stillness
We discovered the embodiment of light and shadow.
The continuous contrast of being made of flesh and bone that wilts and ends
All while pulsating with breath that yearns for another and another.

I will stay here with the Jasmine and the fading aroma of your skin.
Without worry for the seasons continue even when hearts shatter.
We still manage to bloom, again and again.
Petals, ravaged and plagued
Smile in the warmth of the coming sun.

@Michelle.Nicole.Gerrard

God's Justice

Xaku

God's got a way of fixing
People that are broken.

A day in the life
Turned to blessing after blessing
With no words spoken.

Thankful for God's love, so we
Give God devotion.

Sometimes we experience
Foreign emotions.
Spiritual awakening like
An explosion.

Our hearts on ice are
No longer frozen.
We ride the Wave.
Possibilities are wide
Like an ocean.

Trains of change.
Locomotion.

@de_xaku

After E. E. Scott

Courtney Phillips

most days i am a museum of things i want to forget. no scribbled on second-hand maps, no people to guide me. instead taken to see prehistoric things that ache inside my chest, things that should be dead, alive inside my mind, by the hand of heavy eyes and shaking breath. i have a grief everlasting longer than Achilles' love for Patroclus. caged and painted and within every line of dust. every spec. mixed ashes. i have ticket stubs stuck to the pads of my thumbs. and in this moment of being lost inside walls that used to be a home, i wonder why museums immortalize tragedy. most days i am a museum of things i want to forget.

@courtneyphillipsstorytelling

Clare Marie Salokoski

You hold my hand,
As we walk the hill.
I feel I have been here a thousand times,
Holding your hand,
Singing sweet praises of these hills,
Blushing and offering conversation
(I have never been here before).

You hold my hand.
I see birds fly
By invisible breezes
And i imagine bumble bees
Are the violins of flowers,
Serenade.

You hold my hand.

The wind changes,
And we are swept away.
As we lie on this beach,
I trace my finger from sand to stomach,
And the tiny butterflies inside
Fly
I might fly too.
If only I had wings
But today my arms
Have something to hold.

@claremariewithpoetry

Miocene Talisman

Rosemarie Schaut

Fossilized carcharhinidae rests in my purse
while I sit with my mother-in-law in her care home: a place
for lamenting cerebrovascular accidents and where
laughter or even best intentions are scorned.

It hides in my jacket pocket, unnoticed, as I stop to see my
son. Standing in the entryway,
I soothe it between my thumb and index finger,
his fi an cée casually mentioning the leaking roof, a broken
bed, and pricey wedding venues.

It tries to warn me when I visit my mother, knowing her bi-
polar lips will scold me for bringing her donuts, because
"nobody eats donuts in wintertime".

It watches me from my nightstand, counting my husband's
vertebra, and listens to the cursing of his sleep apnea, one
of several angry bedfellows unacknowledged.

Keeping my treasure close, tossed in brackish waters, it
carries me through the middle ages, like a talisman. This
old shark fragment, riding the high tides, to the briny cliffs.

A Winter's Tale (or What Would Shakespeare Do?)
A Modern Tragicomedy

Rosemarie Schaut

Understand
that thirty-four years ago, I did not decide to become a high
school English teacher
Because of my love of technology.

This is what no one tells you --
That you may have to divide yourself, zygotically.
Cells divided for the live classes
Cells multiplied on several screens for those at home.
Students pretending to be present, but who are actually
ghosting,
Playing Halo or Call of Duty,
or feeding the cat.
Showing me their bedroom ceilings,
Their foreheads,
Their Uncle Frank.

Don't forget to record yourself
(--"NOW can you hear me?"
"I think you are muted",
"Does anyone know if Nick will be joining us?"
"Can you see my screen?")
-- for those who are too busy to be here
when you are.

Don't forget to stop recording when the bell rings.

Remember to save, and to store, and to send, and to file,
and to document.

Make sure you are in the hallways during the three minutes
between classes.
Maintain social distancing.
Enforce mask protocol.
Disinfect.
Teach bell to bell.

You may have to contact parents.
Email administration when parents do not respond.
Keep trying.
Date and document your attempts.
Offer grace.

Eat lunch in your classroom.
Do not congregate with colleagues.
If a student, colleague, administrator enters your room
during your lunch, put on your mask
Only eat and drink during lunch.
Maintain social distancing.
Do not leave students unattended to use the restroom.
It is important to stay hydrated.
Keep an open door policy.
Be safe.

We are moving you to a bigger classroom
Because we are increasing your enrollment.
And because your health and safety is important.
Please box up your extensive classroom library for storage.

By Monday.

If you are sick, stay home.
Please do not call in sick. There are no subs.
No one can do what you do.
We appreciate you.
Be grateful you have a job.
Do your job.

Here's a card with a smiley-face in your mailbox.
Appreciate that we are thinking of you.
We are all in this together.

Stay positive.
Students are stressed.
Parents are stressed.
We will not have enough tech devices for all of your face-to-
face students.
Everything must be online for the students who are remote.
Maintain rigor.

Keep an airflow.
Open your windows.
Open your doors,
Wear extra layers.
Speak loudly so everyone can hear.
Remain cautious of internal and external threats.
We will have a drill on Friday.
This drill is confidential.
Be ready.
Windows should be shut. Doors locked.

Prepare your students.

Don't forget to turn on your Smartboard.
Don't forget to turn on your video.
Don't forget to angle your camera.
Don't forget to lock public chat.
Don't forget to unlock private chat.
Make sure students can hear you.
Make sure students can see you.

You must record for asynchronous learners.
Be aware of where you are standing.
Make sure to take accurate attendance.
Email the office if students arrive late.
Record the times in which they logged in.

Students are required to show their faces.
Don't record student's faces.
Speak loudly so everyone can hear.
Engage all learners.

We are still conducting observations.
We are still conducting evaluations.
We are still giving State Exams.
Scores still matter.
Study the data.
Use data to drive instruction.

Meetings immediately follow the final bell.
Follow the one-way traffic arrows in the hallways.
Be prompt.

Make yourself accessible to students and parents.
Remember self-care.

Connect with your students.
Build relationships.
Offer extensions.
Accept late work.
Accept poor work.
Accept excuses.
Accept defeat.

Don't give up.

Remember: we are more than a test score.
Maintain rigor.
Show grace.

No, we cannot purchase that item.
We cannot replace that.
We cannot offer that.
It's not in the budget.
We don't have the resources.
We don't have the money.
We don't have the time.

Work smarter, not harder.
Take care of your health.

P.S You do not yet qualify for a vaccine.
We do not know when you will be eligible for the vaccine.

We appreciate you.
We're all in this together.

@rosemarieschaut

The Last Package

Ryan Sam Turner

i send one last package to your flat,
containing trinkets and letters
from our past -
and i wait and i hope ...

that these souvenirs will trigger something,
which may bring back to you -
all the reasons why we fell in love
and i hope and i wait ...

@ryansamturner

BURNT CHICKEN CURRY TURNS MY MEMORY TO CARCASS

Sezalpreet Kaur

Mom goes out for a walk and tells me turn off the gas in five
minutes. She is making chicken curry and I turn off the gas
in
two hours. The chicken curry is badly burnt; so is the pan
and
when I tell her about this she says it's okay, I'll just have to
clean the dishes. I wanted to tell you I forgot your face
yesterday. Memory is feeble. It keeps getting exhausted. I
wanted to say I'm sorry. Mom makes me clean the dishes
and
my hands are aching and I still do not remember your face.
We
eat burnt chicken curry for dinner and it tastes like cold
metal.
I wanted to remember so much about you. Your hands. The
way you would scold me for burning the dinner. I dream
about
the burnt chicken curry, about asphalt black pan. I dream
about
you. They didn't tell me that you changed your name after
your wedding until I wasn't into my teens. Your name after
your wedding was better, perhaps because you chose it. I
wanted to tell you I forgot your face yesterday. All I
remembered was your brown skin. The mole on your neck.
You scolding me for asking stupid questions about my
English

homework. You standing still in all photographs with dad and
his brothers and your husband. You smiling. You never blinking. You a woman who would've been alive only if our god was a little kinder.

@sezalpreet_kaur_

3 am memories

Lulu Dekey

7:25 am; He was the cup of dark coffee I left untouched on a cold Sunday morning
12:45 pm; He says it's not going to work out... aren't words just cold knives upon warm skin?
1 pm; He kissed me goodbye with blood on his lips. It's a shame he won't do it again
11:11 pm; It's a cold night, I can see the stars. I take an oath under their glowing gaze. Let the constellation bear witness to my secret
3 am... (finally); What is poetry without a little heartbreak and sleepless nights?

@lulu._.dekey

The Fae and I

Tahlia Durrant

Between the chipped and cracked ribs
leaks liquid stardust.

A beacon for inquisitive fae who
contort their twisty spines,
ripping their wings to get a peek.

It would be rude not to offer them
a piece of my brain for their troubles,
as fluttering phalanges poke and prod,
planting seeds that bloom
visions of violets.

Tumbleweed toxins that cloud
the skull make a mean brew
that fills tiny tums.

The sun does rise, crevices run dry.
With full bellies and tired bones, winged
creatures will clear. Leaving behind a
fresh mind within a cavern they
pioneered.

@apricotdaisies

I Was the North Star

kim backalenick escobar

Once, I blazed like the sun
in an autumn blue,
hanging bright against
a robin's egg sky.

I poured myself into
an ocean, becoming the
water that licked
every shore.

I have been painted silk,
lime and sea-foam green,
a luna moth amongst
the gods.

Once, I was the North Star,
shimmering in the cold
thick dark.

Now, I am the light that
lingers on, after the star
is gone.

@edgeofpoetry

Faded Images

Michael Ware

I still remember trips with you
to develop films at Kodak,
you would play your favorite tunes
"If you think you're lonely now" by
Bobby Womack.
Rolling the window down
smelling the city in the whiff,
those memories don't come easy
the older that I get.

Somehow those faded images
that you'd carry in your wallet,
became the foundation of my childhood
and the most important knowledge.
Cheers to you grandpa
those times are not forgotten.

@ware.writes

She Wolf

Jeanie she wrote

She once wrestled
with the wolves
and abandoned the
pack, lassoed wild
villains and arose
from the ash.
She learnt from the
wreckage of the dark
in her life and now her
instincts are relentless,
they only let the light
come inside.

@jeanieshewrote

empty except for these memories
river.

my bones feel hollow now that you are gone
and my skies are always blue
with an undertone of grey
and the songs that play on the radio don't make me
smile anymore
and i think i know
why

i think i know a lot of things
such as why you left,
why you vanished from my life like a moth
flying into a flame and
making it look like an accident
(*we all know it wasn't*)
but in reality, i know
nothing
about you
about life
about
why

and all that is left
in my heart,
that was once filled with nothing
but love for you,
are remnants of a semi-permanent friendship
(*like childhood tattoos: permanent until it's gone*)
and i am empty
except for
these memories

@ascrittoran

Paint me blue

Marie Noelle Aliño

Paint me blue for tear-days
By-the-window days,
loose-hair-blanket-bed days
rub a pale
perwinkle on my cheeks
so when I cup them
I can hold the bottom of my
my blue as if it can be contained
in the smallness of my fingers
dab bluebird on my nose and lips, so I don't only see it but
hear it
so I know it is here again
scrub blue on my forehead so
I have an excuse to go to the bathroom

It might just make me
look at the mirror and
remember only I
can wash the blue away

@bluepaperdays

Scatter that dreaminess

James Kinsella

Dancing under a starry night
Sweet dreams are taking flight
Moonlight glowing with a sweet smile
Stars out peeping behind that smile

I don't want to be alone tonight
Under this moonlight without you
Sprinkle those magical pieces of you
Mixing it with the stardust tonight

Scatter that dreaminess
As we dance under the stars tonight
As we inhale all the magic
The moonlight offers to us tonight

@jim.akinsel.1

On noticing hope

Matthew Lazenby

rise early
Run. Stop.
deep breathing
ignoring the clock
the time it takes
to smell the flowers
crowds move like molasses,
and talk for endless hours
while a soft grip
rocks the baby back and forth
nows not the time
for cursed sleep
or brisk walks
it's only natural
after the year we just saw
to let the lens zoom out
and linger a moment more
then witness the landscape
awash with evergreens
perennials, rolling hills
skies waiting to be seen
soft, ripe fruit
the taste sickly sweet
creaking floorboards
underneath nervous feet
and It surely seems
we're waking up this sound
as we smile from ear to ear,

standing jowl to jowl

@fallow_states.poetry

Bird of Passage

Ell Miller

Bird of passage,
may I join the playful swirl,
the obvious message,
the perfect dance?

Instinctual wisdom,
the fruit of divinity,
for paradise and eternity

Ancestral permeation,
for everything and for nothing,
for forever

Sacred estuary,
allow my vigil;
my humble passing

Bird of passage,
may I join the playful swirl,
the obvious message,
the perfect dance?

@ellmillerpoetry

Twenty Years

Sarah Joannidi

We would sit with strawberry lipgloss
Being passed between us like
Alcohol soon would be
We would speak of the future
Like it were a fairy tale
Not yet aware
that evil step mothers
and deep forests were just around the corner.
When we imagined twenty years from then,
we were babies
And here the years have found us,
with and without our babies.
Twenty years from now,
we'll be a little more lined
a little more wise
But we'll never be snug in glitter and butterfly clips holding
tight to the secrets
That belonged only to us, again.

@Sarah_joannidi

Hemali Mashru

my dreams
sit by the window
flapping their wings,
waiting to fly.
with flying comes
the risk of falling
but i look at the sky
and realise that this wind
is looking for a home too
and maybe my dreams
will find one along.

@toadreamdeferred

Hemali Mashru

on days that my words leave me
i can feel the pain woven on my skin,
slicing through my stomach and
tearing me apart from within.
these phrases melt on my tongue
reminding me of a passion undone
and it makes me wonder if there's
an antidote to remedy this hurt.

@toadreamdeferred

Hemali Mashru

i have become a tide
grabbing fistfuls of air
carrying words like walls
that wash away each time
it rains. tell me, how do you
teach a man what's love
when he's mumbling
a foreign tongue?
i want to become the sea,
take me to a land where
water flows free.

@toadreamdeferred

Jorge Antonio Lopez

when are you coming home?
candle burns at both ends
hot wax seals up eyelids
burn a second baptism
to offer up the sunrise.

wonder what went wrong.
the animals sleep unfed
on a bed of cold earth.
soul thirsts
for warmth
the sun is
delayed again.
when are you coming home?

Becoming a Shadow

Skyler Saunders

I didn't look back. When I saw the chance
to lose all definition, to take the sun and
turn it into a weapon, I ran with it. Before
this I was textbook, the exact middle of the
road, counting down the days until some
twilight would soften the things that made
me cry when I paint myself perfect. But this
bold orange? Me inside, all one shade of
grey brown and only letting you see the
outline? I mean god, I don't have to cover
anything–I can greet the morning naked
and grinning, and you won't see any of my
teeth. Don't think too poorly of me; if you
found a sense of home in the bare living
room walls, I'm sure you'd take it too. I
drew a self-portrait before leaving, hid it
in the couch cushions. I didn't look back.

@skyler.celeste.poetry

Yin to Yang to Yin

Kinza Khan Zimri

This is a serpent's tail and it oscillates amongst itself -
 slithers and slips and back where it started;
 This is a serpent's tail and it knows nothing about eternity:
 how it flows back to itself, how the beginning and end are
one.

The clock ticks: one year, two year, three - things alter
 and things break and things refuse to be - one, two, three.
 I wait, I wait, I wait - how long? How time is a door
 and I stay stuck in it - I wait and I wait and I wait -

Everyone grows tired, the frowns between their eyebrows
 deepen and their eyes sing of apathy and I stop talking;
 but yin to yang to yin, I wait for this serpent to come to
itself;
 how eons are made, how randomness raids -

And cackles a laugh, sloppy witch, says I am here, back
 to take you to what was.
So, they take what is mine and celebrate,
 So, I wait and I wait and I wait.

How time alters, how it is a whim!
 How it brings back what once didn't want to live:
 Yin to yang to yin,
 I take back what was mine to begin with.

@kinza.zimri

Did You Hear What Happened?

Serpico Snelling

Word of mouth / of the river it travels / on a large wet body
retold
In reality a slight / then a falling out / they had to be pulled
apart

Walk the Quaggy / trainers in hand / kingfisher perched on
a shopping trolley
Tell it to the Thames / holder of secrets / no grasses around
here

Shocking whether or not / second son set alight / in tribute
a wall of silence
What a story / retold in mucky pubs for warm beers and
hungry ears
Words in mouth travel always on and on and on

Scarper child / through the tall grass / left at the old
internet mast
Word of mouth / down the river it goes / truth will not be
found
Their life isn't a life / without you / child

@SerpicoSnelling

Grace

Nicholas Cairns

Your imprint still marks me
like a tattoo you'd protest.
You can change the pillowcase
but can't change the head that rests,
for just when I'm on the verge
of forgetting your face,
you come back to me
in a thousand little ways.
I see you on the hillside,
inhale and give chase.
It's both a blessing and a curse;
the most beautiful of wastes.
I'll find you in the place
where memories and absence meet,
where grief in all its grace
puts the sweet in bittersweet.

And for evidence of this
you need only hear
the words I speak aloud,
because when I opened the page,
grabbed my pen and sat down,
this really isn't how
I thought this one would turn out,
but it doesn't surprise me now
that every poem I write
returns to you somehow.

@nik_poetry

Just Dolls

Teodor Nihtianov

in my ill-mapped world of dreams
i seek nothing
but a way out
or how to burrow
further in

and in the failure of both endeavors
I realize the futility
of wanting,
so let the strings dangle
and enjoy the depravity
of the stage

@twistedprusti

Lesbian Haggadah

Ava Silverman

"Be fruitful and multiply."
They thought this sentiment
was meant to apply
to those who walk in straighter lines
to freedom from the ties that bind,
lives defined by normalcy.

If not of narrow type,
if fruity without means of multiplication,
as I, and many others here at this table, are,
belonging is found like afikomen.
We searched for it as children; now we find it at our table.

We gracefully peel oranges.
We spit out the seeds like vitriol;
We are not chametz in this home.

@make_the_flowers_grow

At Night

Zachary J. Ferrara

Sometimes
late at night
when I can't sleep
I read the words of others
to know that
I'm not alone
in the darkness

@zjfwriter

Jennifer McKay

One day at a time,
your body is learning how to feel again.
To feel something besides
the bite that gets the venom out,
the burning coals in the pit of your stomach
and the way they reach into your throat,
yearning painted black

You are learning to want things that are good,
that the best option is not always the hardest
and that sometimes,
the awkward space between
is the room you need to breathe.

Slowly, you're starting to believe
that you deserve good things.
The air around that future
is still soft and foggy,
it is so new that
it can't even see itself yet
but you believe in it.

You believe in a world
that is not fixed, but
a little less broken and
that you will belong there,
that you will know yourself
a little bit more.

When you reach into that space,
the room beneath the door
where something new might be–
you are brave again.
You are the person you're meant to be.

@scentofsnowfall

For Leslie, Pure across time

Jordan Redfern

i save the softest lines for you
the panthers ask me why
and the preachers ask
so does the cavalry of wind
but i tell them
that i hear the sky beat
i hear it cry –
to you i learn to consign the softest lines
may the seas beg me so
and the trees throw a fit
the moon a young lamp
gauche, freshly painted
i will tell the blood brick steps
of my home as a child,
that for you
 i round the stars all up
for you are plenty
shackled and drained the wrist
the wish that yesterday would last
forever

@jlredfern

empty, except for...
Cecilia Bernal

crushing, sharpened knuckles push down on all my
pressure points.
nails get hammered on to try to hold me together,
never expecting to split.
yet when it all gets too heavy,
when i give in and go numb,

you grant me sunspot kisses.
miracle cream on every bruise,
you brush aloe on the burns;
chase cuts in every crevice
and close the calamity.
when i come back to consciousness
the glass fills with your
skin and sensation starts to feel
a little less startling.

@ceciliaabernal

Rejection

Amanda Baker

You still eat the plum despite the pit in the center
The sweetness / the sugar / the juice / the drop that holds
and savors / the slight inclination that the pulp won't kill
you / disease spreads / pain receptors speak / please / pain
won't stay if you are willing to take / the bite / the apple
despite the poison / no core / the core of you is already well
/ and willing to expose once every peel / sheds / the skin
uncovered / all that's left to see / poison gives immunity /
decline me / decline me / down to the seeds / plant me
again / outgrow these weeds / grow even better (not bigger)
/ no matter what / leave me in the center / it makes you,
your best
C R E A T O R

@amandabakerwrites

The bones of a thing

Ian William L.

A storm cannot enter the bones of a thing.
An oak cannot be unplanted.

@ianwilliaml

Sezalpreet Kaur

I keep waiting for you while
I hold a clementine in my
Calloused hands. This is not
A poem but a show of my
Hunger for love, a show of
The widening of the crack in
Everything. In us. I like myself
Only when I'm loved by you.
And when I'm not, I'm an
Anxious child longing
For impossible things.

@sezalpreet_kaur_

The girl you knew

live_inpoetry

The girl you knew is gone
she found herself in you
and your words that rung so true
but she knew her truth was never you

@live_inpoetry

when loving myself meant leaving you
Caitlan Docherty

dirty mustang drumbeat. hooves
    hammer my masterless heart,
rush me to wash

    my bloodstained hands in the melancholy

of shedding old fears.
    it looks like endless beginning,
the tidal confusion of without you.

    salt-laced ocean fire licking the delicate bones

of my feet. shame infused
    across fragile eyelid skin
in tamarind ink, i am
    stuck shut.

@cmnpoetry

GROWN UP GIRLS STILL NEED HUGS
Sophie Cook

What I miss is being able to tell you about my anxieties because you were always a comfort in a way that nobody else was / your body was like a big hot water bottle / that I could hug until I had no strength left / you calmed me down when I panicked over the stupid things / like not being able to sleep and worrying I wouldn't wake up for school / I made sure until I was blue in the face / for you to wake me up / just to wake up anyway by myself / I miss being your little girl down at the beach who could do no wrong / though still annoying / in the arcades / asking for another pound coin so I could change them for two pences / the one choosing out gifts in the shop / usually going for the cute seashells / patterned and shiny / to then ask if I can sit in the back of the van for the journey home / I'd listen to the wheels against the motorway / it always felt like forever but was just an hour you'd say / I miss going to the seafood stall on the weekend / and buying cockles and crabsticks / a weird combination / but I liked the crabsticks in sandwiches with seafood sauce / I don't think you've been taken away / but it just doesn't feel the same / I still listen to songs like 'another one bites the dust' because it reminds me of the funny embarrassment I felt because of how silly you were / I'm too old now to tell you about my anxieties / and what really lingers in my mind / because they're things I'd probably never tell you / I even love listening to kate bush now / can you believe that? / what I remember more than anything / is sitting in silence when you tried to explain why you had to go / and maybe that was the first time I felt heartbroken but now I know even more about heartbreak in different ways / but you're not the person / who is there to hug and comfort me / but I'm still your girl who just wants a hug from her dad / and maybe a trip to the beach would be nice too / or maybe just silence / and it's times like this that I miss hugs from you the most

@WritingSophie

The Pyro Technician

Sam Drury

I was already a volcanic melting pot before you came and poured gasoline into the mix. Fuel to the fire or my willing body thrown into the lava? I burrow my sorrow until it's reached the magma that's on barbecue duty for the first time since last summer. I'm a tricky customer in my own branch of forget-me-not shops. Come on baby, light my fire, so I can melt and run myself through the tube that's nonchalantly hooked up to you. It's twenty-first-century love and it can only get better. I'm hot wax dripping on your naked back, the support act for 'Spontaneous Human Combustion', they're on last and I'm their pyro technician, you won't want to miss them.

@samdrurypoem

That Was Then

Laura C.G

We had a friend on every close: mulberry, hawthorn, walnut, and hazel. The names of trees bearing bounties of fruit and nut. Each day our itinerary would be decided based on which door we should knock. You were hazel. Even then, you were hard to understand, often not up for a race around the block. But we kept you the longest.

And in autumn we'd pluck overripe blackberries from rows of hedges lining the back of suburban houses; ink-purple juice dribbling down our chins, the rest crammed into the basket on the back of your thunder-blue bike. Later, we would watch Disney films on repeat, invent secret societies and magic doors. Gleefully exclude our younger siblings.

I think of those wild blackberries now, left to turn sour, and remember the last time we ever spoke; perhaps we should have eaten all of the blackberries sooner?

@laurabeingawriter

THE GRIND

John Stojevich

yo
ima hit the grind
but i aint got no time
i got money on my mind
though love has taken
all of mine
ill still split the cost
broke off
a lustful star crossed
lovers lost
bill full of liars knots
maybe not today
but maybe i will tonight

yo
this justice dont speak no peace
matter of fact
it acts with a slow
ravishing greed
these streets wreak
of a certain leveled
pale monarchic creed
that to me
seems to be
a concealed form
of slavery
but maybe thats just you
and maybe its just me

ive capture all the sin
that i can live with
have you witnessed
your own reflection
its no stump
into thine eye
much like the splinter
i wear in mine
as mentioned before
i aint got no time
but i hope some love
i can find
its never been a crime
to have money on yo mind
but sometimes to find it
you best get out there
and hit the grind

@johnstojevich

Emily Sun Li

I've been trying for too long to write poems
that move mountains and end wars, that
heal and cleanse and touch and do, that I
can't seem to write anything at all.

So here's a soft poem. A quiet poem.
A silk-petaled lily in your upturned palm.

This poem fits in your hand. It's covered in
the velvet dress of the first girl you loved,
your favorite llama at the Bronx Zoo, your
mother's cashmere sweater. It smells like
lavender and fresh laundry, chocolate chip
cookies, your wife's perfume, jasmine.
This poem tastes like a peach, sweet on the
tongue. Cut and chilled. It feels like
being home for the holidays as a child.
This poem sounds like your sister's voice.
If you're falling asleep, you don't have to listen.

This is my permission-granted poem.
Not every poem has to save the world.
Even Superman gets sick, I imagine.
This poem is gentle and sleepy and sweet.
This is its first day and it's nervous
to meet you. I hope when it apologizes,
you tell it there's nothing to forgive.

@poetry.by.e

Constrictor

Ryan Sam Turner

'i don't love you anymore'

slither ...
her words coil around me
squeeze ...
until i cannot breathe

my bones are breaking
with splintering sounds
my organs bursting
with audible *pops!*

she shuts off my blood -
the oxygen i need
my weak heart stutters
with failing beats

i am now a skeleton sack -
the softest of shells
and that is when ...
she swallows me whole

@ryansamturner

Uninvited Guest

Emily Thomas / Not Much Rhymes With Cancer

And from seemingly nowhere
you made your grand entrance
Peacocking around my body
Loud, proud
Bold, brilliant
Secret, sly

A master of disguise
Sinister in the shadows
Guest of honour at
a masquerade ball
How long had you been hiding?
Leaching goodness

How dare you have been
dancing near my cub
That was one step too far

He never liked you
He gave me clues
He pulled off your mask

Bliss interrupter
Quietness disrupter
Joy snatcher
Sleep now, rest up
Your partying days are over

@notmuchrhymeswithcancer

Tipping Point

Xaku

The sky remained gray
In the hours and days
That my face was poisoned with
Dismay.

It got to a point
Where I was content
To stop fighting.

That point lasted for years,
Lighting
The spark inside me
That kept my sanity
Slipping and sliding.

It seemed like life slapped
Me in the face out of spite.

My imagination took over
While reality kept hiding.

@de_xaku

if music be the food of love, i want you to be here
Jaden Ogwayo

i sit here in the carpark; empty, except for me.
i align my centre of gravity to not fall off
this wooden bench from which my legs dangle.

i hear faint music playing; my background comprised of
beats.
distance muffles the song, but it's avril lavigne; i can hear
her voice.

i open up my phone case; the same as my second-last
customer.
i open up phone and scroll through the red series of
appels manqué displayed in french rouge pixels.

i click on the bottom-left-corner; the favourites' icon:
a star from each constellation, counteracting midnight's
darkness.

i ring you; i don't hear from you.
my loneliness and solitude amplify.
for, despite this carpark as vast as the sky above,
this space is empty, including me.

@jadenwrites

Fair/Faire/Fare

Jen Schneider

I'd braid my hair each evening. Moments before bed.
Freshly washed fingers would weave thick strands of wet
locks. Muscle memory, they called it. Knuckles would
bend, unpolished nails would click. I'd gather, then capture
loose threads. Rebellion - secured tightly. The curls had
minds of their own. Mama said I did, too. Not a fair point,
I'd say. Mama would huff then retreat. No matter. Fingers
with muscle memory met a girl who dwelled daily in the
depths of the night. I'd set my alarm and secure each
braided strand with frayed elastics. I preferred turquoise.
Cranberry, too. Hoped they wouldn't snap. Hoped they'd
last - at least till dawn. Once done, I'd lock my door, turn
off lights, and retrieve my journal from its mattress shield.
Moved with care, to avoid squeaks. Day offered no room for
squeaking. At night, I'd write. Braid recollections of my
days as tightly as the locks on my head.

Bus Fare

At 2 AM on the second Tuesday of each month, the doors of
county jail open. Wide. Teach told us how it's done. Life.
Doors. Re-dos. Some nights, I listen. Closely. I can hear
them. Liked the roar of the downtown train and the whirr
of the uptown airport. Tired bodies shuffle. Timed to avoid
the pain of bright sun on eyes more closely acquainted with
the dark of the night. Timed to avoid the pain of eyes
passing by. Time to thread new paths and pick up

discarded knots. Two tokens - silver, often tarnished - drop
in one of two extended palms. Bus fare.

Fair Weather

I worked today. Minded the children next door. The ones
next to the ones next door came too. Their mama calls it
babysitting, but they're not babies and I didn't sit for more
than a minute. Not even that. No matter. The air was fresh -
slapped me on my right cheek, the sky was blue - color, not
spirit, and the birds were singing - all voices soared. So
lovely.

Fair-y Dust Sprinkles

We spent the afternoon on the driveway. Marking our
territory with upwards of six shades of chalk. Fairydust
sprinkles, offered the oldest as the stick of chalk crumbled.
Ant food, the youngest laughed. Careful now, I cautioned,
ready to clarify - compare and contrast food from fancy.
Mama always said I'd make a ready teacher. A lesson always
in my back pocket. Even when I wore my pocketless skirt.
No matter. Their attention already diverted. The bubbles
floated across the cracked asphalt, tiny spheres of liquid
hope. The children's laughter followed. I didn't know
which to catch, both so sweet.

On Fairing

T. would ask us how we faired the moment the bell rang.
The four of us always studied together. Knew the same

stuff. Immediately after period 1, where we'd identify odd numbers, manipulate variables, solve for X, substitute Y, and reduce all fractions to their lowest common denominator. We'd compare final calculations. The value of X and Y. Then, we'd shuffle - shoulders rubbing shoulders to Period 2. Half of us sent to the room on the right - beakers, test tubes, and periodic tables. The other half to the room on the left - talk of one, two, and three-party governments. Conflict, resolution, dates. Wars of ancient times. Wars of the present.

Bid Facts Farewell

Heads down. Pencils crunch against crisp sheets of lined paper. Aluminum chair legs scratch on tired linoleum. Tired assessments, too. We'd release the well of facts contained and trained. Spill and retell in black and white. Retell and spill on demand. On time. Of time. In time. Names on top. Each page. IDs, too. Minute hands tick. Bells ring. Bodies shuffle. A. finds B. B. grabs C. C had me. How'd you fair, B. would ask the moment the bell rang. The four of us always studied together. Knew the same stuff. No matter - C. always the belle of the ball in Room 4. A. in Room 5. B. struggled. Me, too. Not all ink is judged the same. The four of us always studied together. Knew the same stuff. Stuffed our heads of facts and figures. Figured it might matter.

County Fairs

Teach spent a fair amount of time on homonyms. Words that sound alike but with different meanings. I thought of words like strand. Thread, too. Came up with nothing. Not fair, I thought. Then thought some more. On Mama's coin collecting. Bus fare. The county fair. Town fairs, too. Trade coins for tokens. Games everywhere Odds of winning. Not fair. Yet we'd play.

Fair Game

At 2 PM on the second - first, third, and fourth, too - Tuesday of each month, the doors of the county school open. Most other days, too. Wide. Leather boots, Converse lace-ups, and Adidas slides saunter, then sashay, then run. Most all shoes untied. Blue, green, and red cotton threads cross to form new knots. Ball courts fill. Teams form. Whistles blow. Blue, green, and red floral brush sway in soft wind. Sun would set. Bellies would growl. Alarms would ring. Bid farewell.

--

Some nights, I'd write until dawn. Mama never knew. Such a good girl, she'd say. Early morning sun would knock, then enter. Always before Mama. Without permission, dawn would seize space in thin slots - cracks in, of, over blinded windows. Space my braids would never fit. I should have slept. Should have been sleeping. No fair. No matter. Fingers with muscle memory were trained to braid. To write, too. I'd hear tired bodies shuffle in and out of the hall bath. Claiming all hot water. I'd feel tired, too. Then, I'd rise and ready. Bid the night farewell. Dress for the bus. Dress for the others. Pull-on brown leather boots. Check my locks. Dress the part of the fair maiden. Mama never noticed how tired I'd look. Ready?, she'd say. All locks in place, I'd reply.

[untitled]

Candela Rivero

I forced myself to stay
even when you had left
because it was easier to heal
while believing you would soon
return. I couldn't
let you go because if I did
you would come back
to an empty home.

-I was meant to be your forever home.

@c.r.words

Short Hair

L.G.Chandler

Mum, it's funny really
You're not one for beauty secrets or
Overindulging in luxuries
But with delicate hands
You held the tufts of my fair hair,
My blue eyes full in anticipation,
Creating top-knots and dainty plaits
To show me I can be pretty

Mum, it's funny really
How I went and got the chop,
By the time the tears reached my chin
My hair had stopped,
I despised that bob but you always made fair comment,
Head on my pillow, lights out
Brushing my little ego with a softened blow
I really like it but it will grow back soon

Mum, it's funny really
I spent years wishing for something I didn't have,
Locks to my shoulders (at least) but no
I looked like uncle Martin did in the 1960s,
I despised the bowl around my cheeks so you would say
I really like it but it will grow back soon -
The trims were doing nothing for me,
I was being robbed of my femininity

Mum, it's funny really

You were always right,
Everything does get better over time,
Now my hair grazes
The back of my shoulder blades,
The top-knots and plaits are back again,
You ask me if I like it and I say
I really like it but it's a bastard to maintain

@l.g.chandler

The Wind Blows

David Stant

A star moves across sky's black landscape
A new discovery in the darkness of my mind
As sudden as the star begins to soar
Light calls me within a dream to make a wish

A cool breeze begins to blow
Gently shaping my empty thoughts
And scattering them into a starlit night
In a world within a world

The star descends from the sky
And time moves ever slower
My wish races against an inescapable truth
That I am haunted by the cruelty of chance

When the star nears earth
I wish the strengthening wind
Will carry my fears to safety
Within its soft, subtle embrace

Benbecula

Christian Ward

Thistles trample underfoot.
The Cold War over, missiles
no longer arc like desire.
Wind runs like children
through barracks, shops
and mess halls, slamming
shutters and cupboards.
You remember offering your liquorice
heart to him at the counter,
couldn't find the words when aniseed
rushed to conquer.

*Benbecula is a Scottish island

@christian_ward_writes

A Body, a Tree

Tilly Shore

A white petal falls, it is of the early May bloom,
it is of a blossomed tree

that smothers with the light yielding weight
of its insistence,

that it will be stirred with the gentle wind,
 that a bee can hover, ponder

its hunger for the floweret's soft pink nectar.
And the black body of the bee is a deep night,

its dawn colored wings
are the flutter of old heart strings that are

plucked with the song of children
at their delightful play: shouts(orders);

laughter(independence).
A melody of youth

sung as the spring birds
weave a dance over their bodies.

A deflated shiny balloon is a captive
of the watchful trees with the desert red buds,

their limbs shape

the faces of an ancient spectre,

seen through the snow tints of the wind blown flowers
milling an early May.

Sunday

Melissa Anderson

it's sunday
but to my heart it's tuesday morning
coffee brewing as i rub tired eyes
anxiety percolating in my chest
it's sunday
but my soul roams
the chambers of my heart
looking for a room to call home
it's sunday
but i wander a field with no rain
dry dirt between toes
weeds splayed between rows
it's sunday
but grief came to visit me last night
it fell from my eyes, wet my skin
even though i'd told it not to return again
it's sunday
and i'm coming home

@melissa.anderson.writes

Ham slices

DS Maolalai

making a coffee;
going for milk
from the fridge
and grabbing some ham
while it's open
out of the wet
plastic packet.
folding the slices
and chewing a slice.
going to the window, fingers
to white cup
of coffee. outside, early morning
and a minor collision; a man
standing next
to a quite annoyed bus driver,
examining the dents
on his van.

All my best cries have been at the airport

Laura Mackennon

Dove hands release me into the security line
but there is no wildlife here except the concealed
tastes of home, freeze-dried or globs preserved in jars.

The only way to look out the aeroplane window is wistfully.
One knee curled into yourself like a conch shell.
Like pressing a finger into a square of soft bread.

Scrubbed throat burnt with the memory of white wine
Why must you always drink the night before a flight?
Why must you always drink?
Apparently, planes make you more emotional.
That's why that guy over there is bawling to The Avengers.

The next destination hold all the answers you seek.

Triggered

Sammi Yamashiro

The mid noon sky bleeds out; it bruises in flames.
Arsonists hold their gassers to my face.
In their grisly field of vision, I am a delectable
vapor, born to flit away.
Regard not the orange cones, nor the caution tapes:
these gates hold little significance to them.

(Then the other 'a-word' comes to mind:
anarchists.)

Prior to this, they had presented themselves
as chess pieces to fall in love with–little do they know,
I've an animus for them. As stupid as I may appear,
I know it's a game!

Unzipping out of incognito mode, they have unleashed
their razor blade. They whizz their wings.
Here they come, coming for me.

Here I go again: counting sheep,
blinking for one whole eternity.

Oh doctor! I'm in dire need of your vampiric syringe.
Swill my peaking adrenaline– at this rate, I'll go mad.
I shall never recuperate.

Mollify my entirety.
Teach me to rollick like angels do. I beg you.

@sammiyamashiro

1111

Michelle Nicole Gerrard

1111, my eyes always find the sequences of numbers.
With unspoken love but the words lingering on our lips
My eyes close softly and I make a wish
Always for you
For love doesn't need to be spoken to be felt
Two orbiting beings, wounded and scarred
But with you, Oh with you, I could breathe.
I could feel.
You will forever be the sequence of numbers I never knew I
would grieve.

@Michelle.Nicole.gerrard

Had Things Been Different

Alinda Dickinson Wasner

I might have run off with him
As was my first inclination
But that would have meant
Leaving the children behind
And Spring was in full bloom
The cottonwood spilling its seedlings
(all that "cotton" flying with the bad company
of the willows,
the fluff sticking to our eyes)–

And maybe if the birch trees and alders
Hadn't been shedding
Or the oaks filling with staminate flowers
For the second time and the grasses
Releasing so much pollen
We might not all have been
so completely miserable.

I could have simply disappeared
Mid-morning or evening
The dog in the yard, the children
In the shadows, porch lights
Just coming on
And the seventeen-year cicadas
Ratcheting up their relentless refrains.

Given the right circumstances
I suppose I might have been happier

The sunsets brighter
The days more exotic–

But bring me the books again
That I might reread them
Might find myself on a different page,
Find him somewhere in an adjacent chapter
The corner turned over
My name still emblazoned
On the flyleaf of his heart.

Alinda Dickinson Wasner, Detroit

Conflictions

Carnations and Carnage

I'm either deemed
Beautiful or Repulsive.
But my beauty truly faded
Once I offered you
The last genuine smile
I could give.

@carnationsandcarnage

The Afternoon Cried

Howard Young

The afternoon cried
until early morning
blew in with bitter winds
and dried the empty streets,
someone pulled a red can
off of the wall and
extinguished the fires of laughter
broken bottles cut my feet
as I staggered home, thirsty,

Stooping beneath my apple tree
I held out my hands
in the privileged expectation
of fruits,
but the tree held on fast
a refusal to prove the gravity
of my situation, I thought.

I died down there
at the foot of the tree,
rotted down with autumn leaves
and had my bones kicked about all winter,
picked clean by lazy dogs.

But next spring, to my surprise
a resurrection,
I joined the apples
on the high tree, clinging on,
soaking up the sun
and waiting to fall
again.

@brighton_typewriter_poet

Naked Hotdogs

Brendan De Lucia | Word.Bender

Naked hotdogs expose
the size of the buns.
While corporate pit-bulls
disguise the size of the funds.
Homeless humans are
murdering just for crumbs.
Hungry hippos, the
animals we've become.
Flesh and bone with
an itsy-bitsy skeleton.
I am a silverback spider
hitching rides on gray elephants.
Poisonous ambitions dipping
white fangs into intelligence.
My brown skin is bruised
from all the pangs of
this pestilence.

@Word.Bender

Green Juice
Candela Rivero

I once read that green juice cleanses you
like the human version of a vacuum, releasing
you of your loose lints and leaden lovers. Today, I gulped
two cups yet I can still feel a soreness on the left side
of my ribcage as if your memory clings
to my palate. Cup number one: the superficial
cleansing. Your last words slip down my throat
like burning whiskey. Your face blurs
into celery and you become more digestible.
Cup number two: bitter, brisk, cryptic like
pineapple-tasting spinach and sour lemon
I love you's yet your name lingers
like the after-taste of green juice- the one
that betrayed me into thinking I could ever
be cleansed of you.

@c.r.words

Blue (forever unfinished)

Cait Thomson

When she was first born
her eyes were the darkest blue
the furthest reaches of the ocean
deep and mysterious
a vast universe of futures

Then she turned one
with curious cornflower eyes
that seemed as wide as a prairie sky
limitless and clear
watching over all of the earth

Now she is four
as wise as she's ever been
with eyes bright like an ice-covered lake
home to hidden depths
filled with infinite possibilities

@cait.t.poetry

This Gentle Love
Tom Beck

after Malachi Black

Again the dark light of an evening moon
casts an effervescent light on you,

and following another night of rain
some part of you eludes: you are a brook

inside a bottle: a timid current
convulsing into a still pool

and through: a tiny blade of grass
struggling against the stately trees

that stride upon the wind ... though sadness
falls upon every little breath that moves

your mind, though tears fall on mirrors
of morning grass like dew,

you grow: within your luminous green eyes
all sprouted feelings can be described.

@tombeckwrites

'Oppresserat fames terram'
Jemimah Abigail Hawkes

The ground groaned, scorchedly sore, throughout the
known world;
People came from far and wide to gather wheat
From Egypt's bounteous store, their faces knurled
Around the mouth from water-loss and cruel heat
Which sucked the strength from Man and beast and
unfurled
The deep divisions of the Earth, which now beat
Open the cracked, desiccated ground,
Inviting cries from Many beasts, a sour sound.

@jemimahhawkespoetry

Absence

Rosa G.

Daylight tumbles through the window,
drops of light stuttering through the blinds
and the absence of you
is complete.
Sometimes letting go is seeing what no longer remains,
to holding mornings
like celebrations
little pieces of charred sunsets
hovering
waiting to burn the day again.

@rosa.g.words

Dani Lee

Xaku

They keeping saying,
"If life hands you lemons".

I don't know what it's
Handing me.

After the number the 2,
The hand hits 3.

That's beside the point.

Tired of people
Misunderstanding me.

Shout out to Dani Lee
For being the girl who trusted
Me to be the only man to be
Loyal to her.

I just had to hold her hand to
Feel in my soul that she
Wouldn't abandon me.

@de_xaku

Temporality

Ava Silverman

I found myself nostalgic
for times still yet to come,
missing days that flew in misty haze
while dreaming of better ones.
Writing about tomorrow
while crying over yesterday,
living life in limbo,
floating through each day.

Today, I ate pancakes for breakfast,
and it didn't start a war.

Maybe that's what I've been missing,
what I'm nostalgic for,
the years I lost,
time spent distraught
trying hard to be what I was not,
couldn't see that I was caught
in this seemingly eternal riptide
until I swam to shore.

@make_the_flowers_grow

Afterglow

Nicholas Cairns

Somewhere in the afterglow
there's a place only lovers go.
I've meandered my way there before
but was turned away at the door.

@nik_poetry

Perspective

Teodor Nihtianov

my friend and I were drunk
6'2 and 6'3 respectively
almost thirteen feet
of Slavic frontline shield wielders
throw us to the wolves
and the wolves would die
ha-ha!

and the girl on the side of the bar
was terrified
shameful what this ugly world
did to her mind
white-knuckle grip on the purse,
adrenaline shooting out of her ears
meanwhile there were three cigarettes
in my line of vision
and only one in my mouth

@twistedprusti

the old man who ran away through the fire escape.

Rocío Romero García

i'm on my way home
in a bus that don't have one
and by my side is a girl
reading a book
of an author that i've read
sometime and left in the bookshelf
for writing what i could never,
i don't mind sitting shoulder to shoulder
with strangers
that make me feel protected;
outside is the world
and i can see it
but the only thing that separate me from it
is the window and the priority seats.
in front of me there's a man that reminds me
of the singer that fill my ears
right now,
wearing a peaked cap and headphones
and rings in the fingers
and sometimes we look at each other
as if we met before;
i never notice the hands
but his reminds me of the driver's ones,
rings in the fingers and tie,
as if that justify he has a life
when you get to your bus stop
and you stop seeing him,
maybe you don't see him anymore

and he knows it and wants to stay in your memory and
make you think
he likes to play the guitar
and travel more than just his route
and that he would make the bus his prisoner
if the prisoner wasn't him.
everyday i see people walk from the corner
of my eyes
and when my sight lose them
i wonder if the world lose them too,
if when i turn around they're not gonna
be there
and their only purpose was to appear
in a poem;
today i heard a woman talking about her
platelets,
a man smoking a cigar in the corner
and i imagined his lungs
and the blood of her veins,
i saw an old man coming out a building
with suit and a pyjama in his arms
and an old woman shaking a mop
in the balcony that makes noise with the wind
and i wondered if he had escaped
to go to see her
or if they've ever met,
if that suit was from a youth
along with a summer and eternal love
and if that mop cleaned
the remains of an unrequited love
because it wasn't another one like the old man

who ran away through the fire escape.
i turned and he was still walking
and i saw the earth didn't eat him
and i got happy to know that the earth wasn't plane,
but neither reality.

@losmundosdero

Falling Still

Julius Miranda

I risked the fall
when I jumped into
the unknown
knowing you will
hold my hand, too.
But now, I am
in a perpetual fall
still waiting for your
arms to hold me
while we fly
to tomorrow.

@who_is_julio

Missed Milestones

Ryan Sam Turner

I thought I'd reach all those markers –
the watershed moments supposed to make a life complete.

From a boy to a man –
no more one-night stands.
Find a proper partner, fall in love,
make her my fiancée, later my wife.

We'd turn from renters to owners –
upgrade from a flat to a house.
One child, two ... maybe even three –
a dog or a cat, to complete the family.

But things haven't turned out the way I'd like –
too late now for me to log those milestones.

My existence is quickly passing me by,
my body stiffening, hair turning grey,
becoming more and more lonely
with each turgid, empty day.

@ryansamturner

Natters on the M25

L.G.Chandler

You won't find love when you're looking for it
Mum would say on those
Wild drives down the motorway,
Preaching in a hurry,
Sandwiched in-between two lorries,
Listing veg that would be priority
On next week's shop to the local grocery,
Harping on about the government
And their pickle policies, sorry, *fickle*;
I didn't much listen, too busy panicked by the
Heavy vehicles and our small Nissan in suppression,
Not much would stop this woman

The one phrase,
The only one that would follow with a pause -
You won't find love when you're looking for it -
And on that final lettered stretch,
She'd take the next exit

@l.g.chandler

Reminiscing

Veronika Lukashevich

If childhood had a feeling, I'm certain it would be endless
tanks of energy, the days that seemed eternal, but so did
the heartbreak whenever mum would casually say, "time

for bed now!" She used to be so reckless with my tender, little heart. I would be so excited about the morning that I couldn't fall asleep.

When I think of childhood, I think of flower crowns and pulling the hollow stems of dandelions into long strings, then swirling them in water. The moisture made them look like curly locks of hair that I would put on a short branch and pretend it's a doll.

I think of sharing rooms. For all of my early years, I slept in the same bed as my mother, hugged her from behind all night long, never letting go. So little but always the bigger spoon.

I think of sharing the couch with my best friend in my grandma's tiny flat and stubbornly choosing the side by the wall. I used to secretly run my finger over the embossed wallpaper and push my nail into the print. I could still see the lines when I returned there a few years ago. Some things don't change.

When I think of childhood, I think of bangs, which were my loyal companion, scrunches and coloured tights. I can taste the fresh cherries from the tree in my grandma's garden, sugary black tea and vanilla ice cream from the shop nearby.

Days were long, easy, light. Time stood still, that is what living in the moment felt like. Some days I wish I had never grown up.

@theperfectmigrantpoetry

Dr Yes

Christian Ward

Swap the underwater lair for a Chelsea pad / ditch the manic grin for a lopsided smile / give your henchmen their P45s / dye the white cat a suburban shade of brown / buy a smartphone and invest in Candy Crush until your fingers turn emerald green / tweet / understand youth-speak / abandon the degrees in Psychiatry and Chemistry for something a little media friendly / Pop Psychology and Modern History / become a Tik Tok megastar / make friends with B-listers and embrace the red carpet / sell stories about former lovers to magazines no-one ever buys / look at the stock market and figure out a scheme / charm the lecture circuit and become a prominent speaker / whisper your way to No 10 and advise on defence policy - the sexiest of the lot / never tax or aerospace / draw us to you with a pen / watch our feet hover above the ground / geese taking off at the water's edge.

@christian_ward_writes

Distance

Emily Way-Evans

There is a distance
Between me, myself
And I
Not to far
But far enough
Away
That I can only see
A shadow
Of my former self
Watching me
Across
The void
Since way back when
We parted ways
And promises
Of course
Were made
But then
Life happened
The space
Remained
Even if
I was to try
To find
The silhouette
Left behind
I fear I would
Be swallowed up

By dial up tones
And analogue
This distance
Is a crack in time
This person
Is me
But in the past
Even so
I just can't grasp
How we got
So far apart
And just how much
Time has passed

@emilywaywrites

A Year Ago I Put the Flowers to Death

Kate Kwan

How I did it, I could only remember vaguely:
there was the sound of the leaves being crushed;
the smashing of the petals; and the dirty matter
of removing the soil from the pot.
It was quite a violent scene, though no one could hear it.
The following weeks I mourned.
An inverse crescendo.
I kept counting the days
until I could no longer remember its name–
was it ranunculus, or gardenia?
Or was it some sort of fruits, the nauseous kind that leaves
a horrible smell on your hands
which could only be washed
away by years of deliberate forgetting
and involuntary remembering.
A year ago I put the flowers to death.
Now I realize blossoming only happens
when I kiss you on your deathbed.

@sorsaiwrites

In pieces

Viktoria Schneider

I think I've had too much sex
in too many beds neither mine
nor comfortable
with too many men neither lovers
nor friends.
I think I gave my body away,
betrayed its tenderness
for fleeting moments of connection
with people that would always
stay unfamiliar, *strangers*.
it's way too easy to open your legs
when your heart feels
like it might be closed off forever,
the healing adjourned
by yet another man's touch.
my heart - not an organ but
a comedy of errors, harboring
feelings desperately trying
to deny their own existence.
my body - the graveyard of
emotions floating around inside
what used to be my holy temple
like dead weight.

@jupiterxcrash

Ben Campbell

can i be brutally honest with you?
can i be brutally honest
and tell you that i'm scared sometimes?
sometimes i'm so scared
i will walk through life and
into the firmament
alone
i'm scared that I won't ever form
real attachments to people
that i'll never truly love someone
the way that everyone
should love
someone

because i think i'm better than them
or worse than them
or just *different*
to them

all of them.

i just thought i should tell
somebody

@wordsbybencampbell

A Love Letter To My Body

Emily Thomas /
Not Much Rhymes With Cancer

Body, I'm here
Can you hear me?
You might not recognise me,
i'm louder than before

Body, I know
we've not always been close
There's been some dissonance
despite being written on the same page

But I know you more than ever now

You're not an ornament,
you're a library of self-expression
You're not an object for self-loathing,
you're worthy of worship

You're not just a machine,
you're entwined with nature
You're not autonomous,
you're only whole with mind and soul

This past year, we've grown so much closer

We've created new life with science
and delivered the most precious gift
We've weathered an uncontrolled storm

and dissipated it to nothing

I can hear what you're saying to me now

Body, thank you
From the bottom of our heart
Thank you.
I love you.

@notmuchrhymeswithcancer

girls want
(after maggie smith)
Jax Bulstrode

Girls only want one thing and it's a green velvet couch /
and a thousand days off, and enough time to finish our
book / we want warm banana bread / a night walk / a
house in the forest with tightly locked doors / no
neighbours / a big dog to lay on the end of the bed / to
not be called pretty / to be able to carry pepper spray /
to protect ourselves / to fall in love with another girl
and be able to hold her hand whenever we want / to not
have our body shapes compared to fruit / to wear
whatever we want when it's hot out / to ride the train /
and not have to watch for the shadows / and ask for you
to save us.

@jaxlb1234

MADRE

Michelle Nicole Gerrard

The leaves whispered in the twilight, a tale that wandered
like the seeds of a dandelion on the breeze.
In some far off place, in a time unknown, before I grew old,
I listened to the story of you.

You were a swaying forest tree, and I your sweet wild bird.
With silken soft blue feathers framing eyes that held pieces
of your own.
I found shelter in your branches, my heart at ease as I
nested in your changing leaves.

As the winds began to chill and gales worsened still, there
was peace within the stable home you built. Peace that
softened fear, as golden hour fell, you hummed melodies
that linger still.

Night came and I knew that my heart beat would always
know you. My harbor, my protector, my mother of the
forest green. The one who forever lends her strength so I
can fly, far and wide across the world to discover all that is
new... all that is possible because of you.

@Michelle.Nicole.Gerrard

empty except not

Liv

Crossing fingers I can spit up
itchy sand-covered moments from my frayed body
each year my eyes widen while bushy eyebrows rise
every step I've walked on was a cobblestone cracked
thinking myself into cumbersome circles
a twin to a hamster in a wheel
to be empty except not
begging on bumpy knees to steady
my shoulders with cautious hands
an attempt to grasp on to your smile
like a balloon already inching up towards the moon
maybe I can start healing soon

@notepoemsbyliv

interior-exterior

Cassie Senn

This version of myself is for display purposes only, please just look, no touching. This outline is rusting and I need to form a new exterior in my mind, new lines to form an outer shell that matches with the inside, for I have only been people I am not, none of them at all comfortable. This identity often doesn't feel like mine despite etching my name into my bones, distinct marks on my side, a mortician could identify the body easily by all the scars. Freckles on the outer right wrist, knees damaged from years of hitting pavements and I can draw you a map from memory of all the vandalism and yet it still doesn't quite feel like mine, but at the same time who am I? This external casing is the only source of bodily autonomy I have when my interior is something I don't understand. So sometimes I have to settle for remaining an outline, a container that feels see-through housing nothing but confusion, the yearning to feel like something more than just a magician's illusion.

(saw me in half, make me disappear or levitate, what difference would it make)

@poems.c.h.s

glass human

Tabea von Minden

I'll tell you how this glass human sleeps
She picks up every shard but cuts herself
at it, and tries to forget that she bleeds
I'll show you how this glass human cries
She bottles her tears but spills all the
inside, then waits until every drop dries
I'll explain to you how this glass human burns
She crosses her heart to make it stop
feeling, which lets it still flame up in turns

@potplantpoetry

13 to 30

Begum Elsa Cura

When I was a kid
Not knowing any better
I dreamed of covers that read:
Most beautiful girl!
Princess of the castle!
Look at her style!

Now for my thirties
After all the necessary lessons
They better read:
She stands by her boundaries!
Her career is so unique!
Damn do I respect her!

@thoughtsbyafountain

Untitled

JP Starlin

Can't you feel as
just what is an increment?
can you even feel now–
in fervor garish clicking clock increments?
Feel the incoming of a pouring, torrential rain,
if you'd look inside of you;
you would see a morbid torrid that's so
ready for your New Year's Day all June
and me I cannot say that I'm staunch afraid,
of the time that is unafraid to unwind
should think to be welcoming. so welcome in.
one day each of us all will get–
wisen, ice is, forming
on the tips of your little wings,
but you're no angel, are you?
so you probably don't need those wings
those things,
those parallel universe anything

@j.p.stanzpaul

Punta Di Finale

Simon Wenck

The clatter of plates and cutlery and the overlapping voices
cut out as I closed the door to the common room
and stepped out in front of the wooden cabin.
The glacier at the foot of Similaun reflected the sun's
penetrating beams
as we turned and our attention immediately shifted
to this grey peak
majestically sitting above the cabin's roof.

With a ninety litre backpack weighing us down
we started for that grey peak
and

with
a brief glance at the little stone pyramid
made in remembrance of the Iceman
we continued to place our steps in the
deep footprints in the snow
showing us the way when the red and white
markings on stones and stakes
failed to do so.

Across firn ice and a moraine
we moved our way up the mountain
climbing big slabs while our backpacks slipped towards our
necks
drastically limiting the mobility of our heads.
The only way we knew was up

since the markings left us a long time ago -
so one step at a time
cautiously
we moved towards the summit cross.

We could hear voices, at last
Italian, English, we could hear them
laughing and adjusting their climbing gear
a white helmet, then a red one,
we knew we made it
and greeted this group of four
with a big smile and an even bigger
relief on our faces.

The relief went as fast as it came
as thoughts about the way down
started to infest my brain -
we had to find a new route, one
considerably less dangerous.

Then, suddenly
four ibexes appeared on the west flank
their majestic stride, their prominent
recurved horns and
their calm overawed me

They seemed to study us and
just a few moments later
they started to descend again.

We knew that we had to follow them and

without uttering another word
we trailed them down the slope.

Years later, when I think about it
still with the inability to explain
there is one word repeating in my head:
magic,
magic.

@wordswithsimonx

A Graceful Tragedy

Leon Dunne

"But how did the Angel fall?" I asked
Well, in an effort to understand it all
She tasked herself
To look under every rock and stone
And study all the ants

To feel more, to laugh and cry
To dance until her feet were sore
And sing until her throat was dry

But you see,
They say she simply saw too much
Experienced a glimpse of unrefined infinity
That it sadly changed her mind as such
And gave away her gift of pure divinity.

@Nomanticz

A Lean Fur in the Basilica

LKN

Let me count the bells, with my feet
Along with the loud silence, deafening
My ankles to the numbered resonance
In the smooth cobbled-steps, under me

Tearing the shadows, as the sun sets
At Five, in the south of my footsteps
Clanking the tolls, like a dying ode
Murmured inside, by a parochial woe

As I rise through a descending strung
Of a heartbeat, on a clasping psalm
I had my skewed palm, on each drum
"Thump. Thump. Thump!", says a linger

On my embraced-finger, in a memoriam
Of a flickered-cognizance, held in pauses
That each slither on the cracked stones
Encumbered a cushioned rupture

That my inured soles, are learning a parting
A delayed departure of a behest
As I disembark the penitent landing
"Gasp. Gasp. Gasp!", shrieked a grit

On each pendulous pit, I sojourned
Through the sanctified wreckage, panting
The fated-scriptures, read, by curved

Pronged-lips, bent to a recompense

With each travertine, sculpted bust
Towering like a beckoned shrine
My knelt nape, mounted its skin
To conclave a coveted desire

Yearning the ornate eight bronze panels
To yield, and be begrudgingly flung-out
Behind my awoken neck, to genuflect
A reminiscent entry, to my fagged-memory

Forthwith... a withe fondled my face
To obtrude my gaze, covertly disowned
By the incandescent shadows of bulbs
Hung, like iron caskets, above the pues

Spruced, in its gilded aisles of times, spent
In a paradise lost, in hell's founding
My faculties began to reluctantly pray
"God. God. God!", uttered by a quiescence

While my prescience, moved with my body
Into a procession of an expectant epode
Of my arms dangled, beside my twisted thighs
Beneath the ceiling that seemed like... soaring

While my sights were buried, in a familiarity
An aligning apparition. A pall heave, breathed
Death... sprung on my damp tongue,
Like the birth of an effigy, in a veiled eulogy

Preached in every pinch of paint on the pulpit
Recoiling each timbre to hum; a hymn
Of an unrequited melody; a cacophony
A soul drenched in the nave of a knave

Gave the aversed tarsals, to galavant further
Closer, to the orthogonal gift in the transept
Tarrying the choir of orchestrated halting
As my person twitches, like a severed altar

Succumbed, when the apse squints, in laughter
As my veins felt the ashed edges
Of what seems like a bed; a sanctuary
With an image most macabre, yet... serene

A refraction

@TheLKNPoetry

Regarded Rude and Raw

Cheryll Patras

This crowd of thoughts inside me
has almost swept me away
The noise of the world around me
has deafened me to the core.

In a multitude of summons and
voices I fail to hear the voice I
need to put the puzzle pieces of
my fate and destiny together.

I inquire but nobody responds
I cry but my whispers aren't heard;
probably eavesdropped – but
still, I'm not consoled.

Yea, my yelling is heard all across
the globe by the rooftops and
the human cores –
forever regarded as rude and raw.

@cheryll_patras

Why pissing in a park wearing dungarees is a good metaphor for life

Laura Mackennon

I wear my dungarees in lieu of a personality.
They're storytellers,
shapeshifters
and stereotypes.
Sometimes I'm a DIY enthusiast, paint-flecked
passing time against my rented walls;
practical and focused.
Other times I'm an over-grown toddler,
pocketed hands sulking,
cheeks puffed out like fat cupcakes.
Am I sexy? Probably not.
But I've learnt that the absence of something makes you
want it
all the more.

In Lockdown I live in my dungarees.
Strapping the snappy buckles above my breasts,
ready for a battle
or my daily walk. And they're a great shield.
Great, until
my bladder balloons
threatening to flood my body,
right where I stand,
betrayed and ambushed
in an East London park.

But wild wees are now my forte.

Squat. Legs shaking behind an anemic bush.
Periscope neck with vigilant eyes.
And as I crouch,
it makes me think -
think that pissing in a park whilst wearing dungarees is a
good metaphor for life.
Dropping my denim armour to bare all in such an
undignified manner.
But what a relief
to feel the amber splash back, warm and light against my
tight calves,
a small pool forming on the lightly mudded earth,
to purge the feeling that drowns me, and
makes me squirm and go so small and so quiet.

And when I shake my body like a soggy dog
I look around on the ground and
I see
dozens of muddy craters,
intricate and perfectly formed,
of all those who have peed before me,
the remnants of torn tissues like little white flags, and
I take some small comfort
to know that I am not alone.

Fear Feels Like Wind To Me Now

Elizabeth Lerman

It's 1:06am and I am sitting on the subway wondering if tomorrow night, when we are in that big house, with all that empty land, her ex will kill us. He probably won't. She thinks he won't but she also didn't think he would hit her. I have underestimated his type of anger before, I know, so I can't help but watch while a scene plays out on the inside of my eyelids, a scene set against snow and something solid, something familiar, a scene that scoops up all sense of safety I ever might have felt up there, in that once trusted tundra, and scatters it into the air. And fear feels like wind to me now because hasn't it been behind us our whole lives and haven't I rocked and swayed with this feeling for a reason? Maybe not, maybe I'm paranoid and maybe I'm scared of everything but maybe I know that angry men, pitiful men, can do shocking things, and really the things they do aren't even that shocking anymore because we see it on the news all the time and we see the dead wives and the friends who never saw it coming and I'm thinking, what if they did see it coming? What if I saw it coming and what if I felt it in the wind and maybe I'm paranoid and maybe I'm scared of everything but how can I not be when we keep dying for saying enough, for saying stop, I'm done, for saying I'm leaving and slamming the door behind you and you, I'm talking to you now, you who thinks he won't do it, did you think he would hit you? If I had asked you, before it happened, what would you say the percentage would have been, of him hurting you like that? Low, probably, I would have thought low, but he did and I learned to stop underestimating a weak man's anger. From what I can see, hurting you seems to be his only hobby, so maybe I'm paranoid and maybe I'm scared of everything but look at me with all of you and tell me why I shouldn't be.

@ebl.writing

Drowning in nostalgia

Camilia Aaliyah

The sun is waking up
and I've yet to sleep
for you I'm falling deep
nostalgia washes over me
and I choose not to swim

I catch the sunrise
and watch as the sky
fills with the colors
you painted my life with

And when the morning sun
kisses my skin
I think of the warmth
you made me feel within
even on the coldest days
with you I felt the sun's rays

@bleeding_poetry

How's Life Been?

Sammi Yamashiro

It sat on my lap again:
the unavailing programming jumpstarting the jibberish
coding.

I should labor at my nine-to-five, plan out my meals
to nibble thrice a day, and do as we do.
I'm reawakened. The stimuli is inescapable.
I'm brought up to be simple-minded, to pretend
I'm a luxury car zipping through the country-wide bridge.

Oh, the curious! The eclectic!
You progress our technologies and yet
your nature is rebellious.
I'm aware of the trickery.
Perhaps my final genie wish is to revert
to obliviousness.

When such is the predicament,
how can you expect a decorated answer
to the trite, battered-up greeting:

How are you?

I'm fine. Dandy.
Life's ushering as it should.

Do what you will with my response, oh stranger.

@sammiyamashiro

The Mother

Catherine Hamilton

I created an exquisite work of art
Crafted from gem stones and gold dust
Gilded in pieces of my heart

Thumbprints of love remain
As I sculpt to absolute perfection
Preparing for what is to come

Gripped in fear I wonder why I did it
Why create something so beautiful
for a world so ugly

I want to build a gallery
An empty exhibit admired only by me
Safe from those that will chip at its brilliance

Instead, I ready my tools.

@cathamcreates

The Last Moment

Emily Thomas /
Not Much Rhymes With Cancer

A warm breeze
sweeps over my face
Autumn sun soaking
into my skin

Hazy lavender
sways softly
Conducted by
batons of buds

The hum of bees
vibrates in the air
Soothing my
thumping heart

Faces emerge
from the dark cave
Happy and relieved
Sad and destroyed

Nature quietens
the terror
The last moment
before the noise

@notmuchrhymeswithcancer

Leah Fricke

I could
wrap myself
tightly
in parachute cords:
braid them
carefully
around my waist
and call it safety.
Is it not
meaningless
without the
freefall?

@when.sunshine.rains

Isabelle Chow

There are years in me that have not slept
mornings so late that it's early
from when life put the strife into me

There are tears in me that have yet to be wept
mourning and self-hate
from when life took the life out of me

There are fears in me that I just can't accept
morphing into different scenarios
but all having the same outcome
of regression and depression
of regression into depression

There are times when I wonder
if people are really coping
or just charading around with the illusion of reality
and parading around with the delusion of normality

@singing_scratchpoet

Gazing out the window at 10 a.m.

David R. McIntyre

I take great pleasure
in the moments of unperturbed
graceful silence.
A few stolen fractions
of daylight.
Even on the dreary days
and with the withered leaves
the trees still look good.
If this is their hangover
then let them feel it.
We are all the same in the eyes
of the Moon.
Anyway.

@sisterkind

Marked

lydia falls

i can't seem to find
those teeny tiny
footprints
(the ones he left
down my spine).

if i wander without
those teeny tiny
footprints,
i'll be bare-boned—
they're essential.

just give me another day
(sometime, shortly, soon).
they're teeny tiny,
those traces along my skin.
his are sure to fade.

@lydiafalls_

A poet is a poet.

David R. McIntyre

A poet without doubt
is a tree without wind.
No threat of being overwhelmed
by a cataclysmic storm.
No chance to develop that
strong stress wood spine
to remain upright
when life refuses to rhyme.

A poet without heart
is a bare canvas
for others to paint meaning on
image over image
of two dimensional
sadness.

A poet without a soul
is viciously deceptive
at once damned
with the essence of spirit
yet roam blessed
feeling none of it.

@sisterkind

what i wonder and what i remember

Jaden Ogwayo

part 1. the city

i wonder how it feels to interact with strangers without ever questioning the role your identity plays. i remember code-switching before i learnt of the term. i remember serving customers after a football match and being told by a couple that "you need to watch it if you really want to seem like a true australian". i wonder how it feels to voice concern without needing to excessively sugarcoat your feelings to avoid being discredited. i remember the wave of anxiety when walking past a police car and changing how i walk to avoid suspicion. i remember how i monitor my behaviour: no swear words (too angry), walk slower (running is a threat). i wonder how it feels to walk past officers and maintain the same mannerisms. i remember hearing a security guard tell a white teen who stole that he'll "be nice and won't arrest" him. i remember my friend telling me of her brother's encounters with police: less justified; more brutal. i remember saving instagram infographics to learn about my rights and for advice on dealing with an officer. i remember reading xenophobic graphic t-shirts on a customer in my store's front queue. i wonder how social media feeds look without the reminders that people your age, class, and colour experience violence at the hand of police and the state.

part 2. the classroom

i wonder how it would feel to have an assignment on bigotry before you've experienced it. i remember being assessed on how i voiced personal experiences; graded on how i sanitised my language and pain for palatability's sake. i wonder how it would feel to require thorough research to discover a social system so foreign to you that you can only observe it through wikipedia hyperlinks and google news headlines. i remember awaiting the inevitable reprimand for minor actions in front of a class doing the same thing. i remember the astounded relief teacher telling me "wow, your english skills are really good. how did you learn?" after answering her questions. i wonder how it would feel to speak your native language unquestioned. i remember having my rights debated in a classroom. i wonder how i stuck out to others in my years of being the (l)on(e)ly black kid in several classes. i remember researching examples of persecution based on an identity i shared. i wonder how it feels to find pages of people who look like you in history textbooks. i wonder how it feels to have a person that inspires you whom you resemble. i remember always picking "obama"; the only man; my single choice.

@jadenwrites

Ego

Lisa Simpson

Whipped pale grey billows and ruffles her
soft folds of silenced feathers.
She tumbles and rolls
gently as downcast sighs drift by,
spurned by those who seek gold and
tinkling melodies.
She quietly waters her fragile shoots as they unfurl and
raise their heads above the crumbling earth
and wait, greedy mouths agape.
And as they grow and bloom and dreamers be,
shrouded in night's veil where no one sees,
she sways and drums as her delicate ones
drift in slumber on a fluttering breeze.
Her gentle rhythmic tapping soothes
budding little heads, glistening, awash with her moonlit
scent
and listening to her constant beat,
their constant. Their sweet comfort.

@afewwordsofmine

joie de vivre

Corey Bowen

my loves only know
broken ends.
a new one each season,
four flavors that linger
on my tongue, but never
for long enough
and never without regrets.

@coreylectron

Isle of Flightless Birds

Atlas W. Keeting

We,
the talking heads,
the bobbing knobs,
the squawking kings and queens have
stayed too long, played too rough, and ate too much;
and now,
on this isle of flightless birds,
we have seen better days,
and we have become the victims of our own creations,
so excuse us while we sing
to the sky and dream of flight
on this ravaged, bare isle.

@atlaskeeting

Fearful Waiting

Sare Chafin

I used to wait on the playground after school
watching the parents arrive,
scared that you would find me
and whisk me away where my mom
would never think to look,
but curiosity balanced fear.
I wanted to know if I looked like you.
if I was evil like you.
if you thought about me, like I did you.
but the question that clung to me
for years after I tried to shake it off
was - why didn't you love me, like I
wanted to love you?

@sarechafin

Seasonal Musings

David R. McIntyre

There is an intuition to the seasons.
The way they seem to know when to come and go.
Havering mad isolated metaphorical angst
and grown out stubble meets their older self
who is younger than them.
Blissed out fever dreams indigo skin under sunbeams.
Reminiscent of joints at the igloo and the dogwalkers
chastising stare.
Humble of the rain to pour somewhere else for a change.
Wonder if they ever consider our effort
or do they just sit there and snigger?

@sisterkind

An Ode to the Sunlight's Sad Beauty

Erin Cherie

Chasing the tail of tomorrow again,
it's my sour-faced sweet speciality,
with my pride stumbling over its feet,
shedding layers and leaving my body.

An ode to the sunlight's sad beauty,
here's what I get for my dark curiosity,
a boat washed up, broken and rotting;
maybe its muscle memory will hold me.

@erincheriepoetry

a love song made out of toothpaste

Mina Lucania

i gargle a love song
and i spit it out
with the toothpaste
the faucet is leaking and i'm too scared to
make a phone call

i've never spoken to a plumber before
i don't know what you're supposed to say

you're not a plumber so i hope you won't take offense
i'm not scared of plumbers i'm just scared of calls
i'm also scared of calling you in case you don't pick up
and it's because you died or worse because you
don't want to hear my voice

i realize i'm exhausting

like the drip drip drip of a
leaking faucet
and i test your patience i put so much effort
into being the worst
i know you know that
you appreciate the effort

still you might leave anytime and i can't stop
reminding you and myself that
every word i've ever said meant that i wanted
you to stay

but they all come out gargled and stale like puddle water
and i don't know
if you understand exactly what i mean
when i say can you call the plumber i'm too busy today
i'm afraid you don't understand me at all

and if you can't even understand what i mean when i say
please call the plumber
i don't know if you'll ever understand
how many love songs i've sung to you
while i waited
for you to pick up the phone

@mina_lucania

Paper Planes

Zara Al-Noah

We each take a piece of paper
from under the retired stove,
pass it to one another.
We smother our recycled sheets
in remnants of bold
crayons, and massage petals
of orchids and plumerias in circles,
thieving scents of saccharine
growth for flight.

I recall the angles and creases, feeling
my Father's hands atop of mine, and
hammer down my guilt that you
never knew yours.

Your little hands mimic me at my side,
so I fold slowly, and with each fold
I emphatically entrench everything
we have learned from each other,
how much love we both have to give.

We fling open the window and admire
the trajectory of our efforts, our mutual
adorations swooping July's humidity,
our twirling excitement willing them
to catch thermals, wishing them
a safe journey.

I tousle your silky hair, cherishing
a dream for your future,
a world peppered with paper planes.
But all I say is,
"there is no limit to how many
your sky can hold."

@littlepocketpoems

Jessica Huddy

I stay out of the way
of the kitchen drawer

stick my two cents back in my pocket
where they belong

turn a blind eye
one cheek after another

tuck my hair behind my head
with all my hard feelings

@j.l.huddy

Someone who never quit

Simon E. Northcott

I went down the Regent's Canal
today, it was such a glorious day,
I looked at those house-boats
floating on the water, their
lodgers looked so cool, painting
boards red and blue, having coffee,
eating bacon muffins, selling junk
or homegrown plants, rosemary and
sage, takings pictures and talking
to the passers by.

I thought to buy one, then pray
for a storm, a tzunami,
the Great Flood: something that
made me sink and drown while asleep
like a true Captain with his ships.

People, for once, would've thought
that I was someone who never quit.

@simone.northcott

Guest House

Karina Kupp

my body is a guest house for lazy ideas
they arrive, have fun, talk loud
and leave to never return
paying me with a number of sleepless nights
when I think about what it would be like
if I was a long-term rental

@mutedpoems

Haiku - Free

Elaine T. Stockdale

A field of bluebells
running with the breeze, and I
wish to be as free.

@e.tstockdale_

Lost In The Supermarket

Howard Young

Lying there, all alone, unmoved, almost elderly
Dyed hair, lying on her back and looking up,
Without a care for things that happen around her.
The trolleys whisk and whizz
Sharp voices rattle back from the modern walls
But she remains, A woman quite small
Texting, or looking up the weather,
Or whether the best deals 'Here in store'
Are really here at all.

Two ladies, middle aged in hygiene hats hover,
Assistants looking for assistance
For the woman, as one reassuring smile is
Swapped for another.
What to do next? The tills are not covered and there is a
small queue, but a woman lies, in the centre of the lobby
Where they serve coffee, to no one right now.

The woman still smiles like half a cake
scrolling and scrolling away,
as a manager, firm but fair, arrives
The two assistants slide away
to the cake coffee counter,
Ten minutes later, while the woman prostrate
Beside her empty shopping bags
Stranded like a broken albatross
Her 'react to light' sunglasses staring to clear

Her blue grey eyes slowly appear
And the manager, hands on hips in the entrance hall
Elbows like flying buttresses, makes the emergency call.

A staring crowd gathers in a slow mutter
The story ends as I walk outside, the ambulance arrives
And though I don't wait
I bet as she was wheeled off to a waiting bed
She was checking her phone
Living or dead.

@brighton_typewriter_poet

Index